BECOMING AN ACADEMIC WRITER

Dedicated to the Author of my life's story,
who penned in blood ink the happiest of all endings.

BECOMING AN ACADEMIC WRITER

50 Exercises for Paced, Productive, and Powerful Writing

PATRICIA GOODSON
Texas A&M University

Los Angeles | London | New Delhi
Singapore | Washington DC

Los Angeles | London | New Delhi
Singapore | Washington DC

FOR INFORMATION:

SAGE Publications, Inc.
2455 Teller Road
Thousand Oaks, California 91320
E-mail: order@sagepub.com

SAGE Publications Ltd.
1 Oliver's Yard
55 City Road
London, EC1Y 1SP
United Kingdom

SAGE Publications India Pvt. Ltd.
B 1/I 1 Mohan Cooperative Industrial Area
Mathura Road, New Delhi 110 044
India

SAGE Publications Asia-Pacific Pte. Ltd.
3 Church Street
#10-04 Samsung Hub
Singapore 049483

Acquisitions Editor: Vicki Knight
Associate Editor: Lauren Habib
Editorial Assistant: Kalie Koscielak
Production Editor: Libby Larson
Copy Editor: Megan Granger
Typesetter: Hurix Systems Pvt. Ltd.
Proofreader: Christine Dahlin
Indexer: Jean Casalegno
Cover Designer: Candice Harman
Marketing Manager: Helen Salmon
Permissions Editor: Adele Hutchinson

Printed in the United States of America

Library of Congress Cataloging-in-Publication Data

Goodson, Patricia, 1958-

Becoming an academic writer : 50 exercises for paced, productive, and
powerful writing / Patricia Goodson.

p. cm.

Includes bibliographical references and index.

ISBN 978-1-4522-0386-7 (pbk.)

1. English language—Rhetoric. 2. Report writing.
3. Academic writing. I.
Title.

PE1408.G585 2013

808′.042—dc23

2011048279

This book is printed on acid-free paper.

12 13 14 15 10 9 8 7 6 5 4 3 2 1

Brief Contents

Detailed Contents

Figures and Tables

Preface

I never imagined writing a book like this. Yet here we are, this book and I, attempting to motivate you to write more, write better, and publish your academic work. I can't help but feel both wonder and surprise when I reflect on the journey that led us here.

One reason I never expected to write such a book lies in my professional training. Having started my career in linguistics, I eventually found an academic home in health education and a research specialty in adolescent sexuality. While I managed to sustain an interest in all things language related, prior to this book, my academic writing comprised reports on evaluations of sex education programs, development of new contraceptives, and studies of adolescents' sexuality. My previous book critiqued current health behavior theories; it had little to do with language or writing, except for the approach I employed. In that text, I challenged readers to view social science theories as stories, as narratives written by scholars to explain why people do what they do.

So how did I revert to my linguistic origins and come to write *this* book? Primarily as a result of working for several years with graduate students and junior faculty, sharing the tools and tips that impacted *my own* professional writing.

Before I started learning and applying the ideas I present here, I was a somewhat competent writer. I enjoyed writing, recognized how important it was for academic success, and published at a slow-but-steady pace. It wasn't until I began practicing the strategies I spell out in the chapters you are about to read, however, that my writing blossomed in consistency, productivity, and quality. Only then did I become more and more excited about writing and start relishing the writing process.

As I learned, practiced, and saw the positive outcomes in my own writing, I became convinced *anyone can write*—as long as they learn the steps to developing a healthy writing habit. I couldn't help, therefore, but share with each of my graduate students what worked so well for me. As I shared, I watched in wonder how what I taught impacted their writing as powerfully as it had affected my own. Working with them, too, I became convinced of yet another important truth: The most important tool for academic success is the ability to write and publish; graduate programs that are not helping students develop a healthy writing habit are doing their students a disservice. I had unexpectedly stumbled on a gaping hole in graduate education, an urgent need.

Need and opportunity converged at precisely the right moment when I was invited to work with the graduate studies' development initiative in my college (another unexpected turn in my academic career). To enhance the training experience for our graduate students, I created a peer-led writing-support system named POWER Services (Promoting Outstanding Writing for Excellence in Research). Developing and honing POWER Services—which include teaching a college-wide writing productivity course—led to meeting the urgent need I described above, and eventually led to this book.

Teaching writing productivity courses and directing POWER Services forced me to develop and accumulate many tips and recommendations for productive writing. What better way to organize all these strategies than in a book?—after all, doesn't the acronym BOOK stand for "basis of organized knowledge"? As I considered the idea, however, I also was keenly aware that merely assembling tips and tools, no matter how well organized, would not be enough to convince readers the recommendations would *work for them*. To persuade an academic audience these strategies were valid would require a scaffold of both theory and research answering the question, "*Why* do some tips I practice improve my writing productivity while others do not?"

The search for answers led, unexpectedly, to the notion of deep practice, the psychology literature on expert performance, and the neuroscience behind the development of talent. Coupled with Peter Elbow's writing theory, these elements became the platform I needed to structure the tips and suggestions into a book. I was ready to write.

I wrote driven by a sense of urgency and immediacy, need and opportunity, surprised that I was actually writing the book I had never imagined writing. And as I placed words next to each other and sentences one after another (isn't this the essence of writing: one word at a time?), those feelings of wonder and surprise kept me asking, repeatedly: Me, a successful, productive academic writer? Me, helping others write? Me, who breathes theory, dreams prevention, and practices learning, pointing the way to excellence in writing? Who would have thought? I certainly never would have expected that investing in my academic writing would one day return me to my linguistic roots, lead me to unexpected places, and compel me to write this book.

That's the short version of how we got here, this book and I, and now that you know why I wrote it, it's time to turn to your own writing. But before you start, a brief warning: As you work through the exercises and invest in your academic writing and as you write more, write better, and become a prolific author, beware of potential side effects. The most serious will be the many episodes of pleasant surprises and positive outcomes resulting from these efforts. Among these surprises might be, perhaps, that one book, journal article, or piece of writing you never imagined writing! So, proceed with care, expect surprises, and enjoy the results.

How to Use This Book

I designed this text as a workbook for use on a daily (or regular) basis. You can adopt it as a self-paced workout, or, if you teach writing courses or work with writing groups, you may assign specific chapters to be read and practiced over a certain time period. I guess by now you know who I had in mind as the intended audience for this book: anyone in an academic setting who must write to survive—specifically, graduate students, postdocs, or junior faculty. This doesn't mean the book can't be useful for undergraduate students, or even for writers outside academia. The audience I initially had in mind as I wrote these exercises, however, consisted of my *own* graduate students and faculty colleagues (keep in mind, these folks are either in education, social sciences, or public health). That I was writing for my students and colleagues explains, to some extent, the informal, conversational tone I employ throughout the book.

The book begins with a brief theoretical and empirical grounding of the exercises I propose (Chapter 1). It follows with 50 exercises (Chapters 2–11) designed to help you establish and maintain a writing habit, as well as progress through the stages of writing a journal article or research proposal.

If you're using this as a self-paced workbook, you can sail through all 50 exercises during a year, focusing on one exercise per week with a 2-week vacation (yes, *rest* is an important element in structured practice, even for elite performers). You can choose to practice them more quickly, if you'd like, but keep in mind the need for *practicing*, which implies *repeating* the exercises.

One way to use the book is to start with Chapter 1 and work your way through Chapter 11. Depending on what your needs are at the moment, however, you may choose to begin with any chapter and skip around. Whichever approach you pick, remember, it's best to do the exercises *within a given chapter* in sequence. Several exercises build on those practiced earlier and depend on previously developed skills. I also think it's a good idea to read Chapters 1 and 2 before you tackle any other chapter, because these chapters prepare the soil in which you will plant the writing-productivity seed: a healthy writing habit. Absent this habit, the idea of practicing writing regularly becomes sort of like weeds in your garden—a sheer nuisance.

After you have chosen a chapter, commit to starting with the first exercise and working your way in sequence to the last exercise in that chapter. You should practice one exercise per week and repeat it several times—preferably at the start of every writing session. Remember, the more you practice, the better you will become. But the idea is not to overwhelm yourself with practice or to become tired or bored with it. That's why the exercises are designed to be brief, so you can repeat them several times and not wear yourself out. Most exercises require merely 5 to 10 minutes of practice.

What to Expect

Let me begin by telling you what *not* to expect: Don't expect a miracle, please! By miracle, I mean, don't expect your writing habits to change overnight and book publishers to come pounding at your door begging for your writing expertise. And although this book is grounded in the notion of deep or deliberate practice—a crucial factor in the development of out-standing talent and extraordinary competence—don't expect to become an elite performer in 1 or 2 weeks, either. If this is what you anticipate, you are setting yourself up for serious disappointment. A well-known rule of thumb among expert performers and people with outstanding talent is the 10/10,000 rule: It takes about 10 years or 10,000 hours of practice to develop out-of-the-ordinary expertise.

Even for the best and most productive writers, therefore, the going is slow, the labor is intensive, and the need to rewrite is nonnegotiable. I share Anne Lamott's (1994)[1] sentiments here:

> I wish I had a secret I could let you in on, some formula my father passed on to me in a whisper just before he died, some code word that has enabled me to sit at my desk and land flights of creative inspiration like an air-traffic con-troller. But I don't. All I know is that the process is pretty much the same for almost everyone I know. The good news is that some days it feels like you just have to keep getting out of your own way so that whatever it is that wants to be written can use you to write it. . . . But the bad news is that if you're at all like me, you'll probably read over what you've written and spend the rest of

the day obsessing, and praying that you do not die before you can completely rewrite or destroy what you have written, lest the eagerly waiting world learn how bad your first drafts are. (pp. 7–8)

Realistically, expect your first drafts always to be bad, even if you become a ridiculously productive writer. If you keep practicing regularly, however, you can also expect to develop a writing *habit*. This habit will lead to improved quantity and quality of writing and to less stress during the writing process, more myelin around your neurons, and more papers in your curriculum vitae. With time, believe it or not, it may also lead to better first drafts!

I cannot *guarantee* these expected improvements for everyone, but I can *almost* guarantee them. The reason I cannot guarantee they will work for you is because I won't know how faithfully you practiced the exercises, how thoroughly you completed each one, or how willingly you stuck to the exercise plan. What I *can* guarantee with absolute confidence is that you won't achieve these improvements if you don't practice. I would bet my whole salary on this! However, I have learned from personal experience, have heard enough testimonials from my students, and have read enough before-and-after papers that I cannot ignore the power inherent in the principles and practices offered in this book. I have seen how transformational these strategies can be in the writing lives of many, many students and faculty, so I can't help but feel certain they will work for you, too!

Regarding the book's structure, expect this: Chapter 1 introduces the model that grounds the exercises. Part I comprises five chapters (Chapters 2–6) with 28 exercises to enhance the productivity and quality of your writing, in general. These exercises can be helpful for almost everyone in an academic setting. Part II contains five chapters (Chapters 7–11) with 22 exercises designed specifically to help you practice writing portions of academic papers such as introductions, methods, and discussions. Keep in mind that I discuss these specific sections of academic papers (and grant proposals) within the context of the social and behavioral sciences, my academic home. If you are not in social sciences, some of my recommendations will not apply directly to you, but you will still learn a number of useful tricks from the chapters in the second half of the book. The book ends with an afterword, in which I present my final thoughts and challenges for you.

Some chapters contain "Tips for ESL Writers," and all chapters present a call-out box with snippets of research on academics' writing productivity. As you read the research data, I believe you will gain greater confidence in what you're doing and a stronger sense that this notion of practicing writing is valid and reliable. Expect, too, to learn some interesting findings uncovered by this research!

In the Appendix, I have placed a resource list with other books and websites to help you with your writing. Finally, on the book's website, you will find templates and logs or matrices you can use to keep track of and organize your work. To access these, go to www.sagepub.com/goodson.

A Note for English-as-a-Second-Language (ESL) Writers

If English is not your first language, you will also find this book useful because I provide a few tips especially for you. My experience teaching academic writing to nonnative-English-speaking graduate students has offered a few lessons about what works and what doesn't work to facilitate your academic writing. Therefore, interspersed throughout the text, I suggest different exercises or variations on already described exercises, which will benefit ESL writers in particular.

Feedback

This book is a work in progress, as I continue to learn about and craft new strategies to facilitate writing productivity and enhance writing quality. Because this work is a living, dynamic piece, I need to continue feeding it with input from *you*, the reader. If you have suggestions for improving this text, please feel free to contact me and share your recommendations. Nothing would be more delightful than to learn how you have used this book and how helpful (or not) it has been for *you*. Feel free to contact me by e-mail at goodsonworkbook@gmail.com and let me know what you think.

Pat Goodson
College Station, Texas, 2011

Note

1. Lamott, A. (1994). *Bird by bird: Some instructions on writing and life.* New York: Anchor Books.

Acknowledgments

While writing this book, I received countless gifts wrapped in social, emotional, and instrumental support, from many people—and without these (the support and the people), I would not have written a single word. Well . . . maybe I would have, out of sheer stubbornness, but then the writing would have felt like . . . well, like *work*. Instead, these support gifts—joy upon joy piled high—made the writing feel more like *play*. Therefore, to everyone who contributed to the many playful and joyful moments, I am truly grateful.

Yet I must single out certain people for a *special* thank you, because without them, I wouldn't have *completed* this book—no matter *what* the writing felt like. First, I am very grateful to Dr. Doug Palmer, dean of the College of Education and Human Development at Texas A&M University. Were it not for his vision, POWER Services would have remained merely a good idea. Instead, because of his support and investment, many graduate students in the college have benefited from the writing model described in this book. Several students have shared with me that practicing this model changed their academic lives forever; others have admitted the model saved their academic careers, as they were about to drop out of graduate school due to struggles with writing before they began practicing the suggestions I offer in the book.

In my department—Health & Kinesiology—Dr. Richard Kreider (the department head) and the chair of my program, Dr. Danny Ballard, facilitated my investment in POWER Services, at the expense of some of my duties within the department and the program. This book is a testament to these administrators' belief in the importance of providing writing skills to graduate students, despite the costs.

Along with the structural support I received, I could not have completed this project without the steady encouragement from people with whom I shared my writing efforts on a weekly, and sometimes daily, basis: Keara O'Dempsey (even though we haven't yet met in person, she offered the opportunity to report my writing online every day and gently kept me on track), Erin McTigue, Laura Stough, and Sandra Acosta (faculty colleagues at Texas A&M, with whom I exchanged weekly reports). In addition to these faithful supporters, I also counted on several outstanding POWER Services consultants who read portions of the manuscript and offered precious reader-type feedback whenever I needed it. No one could dream up a better support team!

A special word of thanks goes to my colleague Yvonna Lincoln, who graciously introduced me to SAGE Publications. At SAGE, I had the privilege of working with Vicki Knight, who shared my vision for this book from the start. Her support, expertise, and professionalism added a touch of class to the editing and publishing processes. I am also thankful to Libby Larson at SAGE for help with production, to Megan Granger for the kindest copyediting an author could ever hope for, and to the seven reviewers who commented on the book proposal and the manuscript— definitely some of the most useful feedback I received! My heartfelt thanks, therefore, to Carol A. Kochhar-Bryant (The George Washington University), Kathleen Bobay (Marquette University), H. Elisabeth Ellington (Chadron State College), Sarah Baker (George Mason University), Tonette S. Rocco (Florida International University), Laura Huntoon (University of Arizona), Tanya Maria Golash-Boza (University of Kansas), Eric Hadley-Ives (University of Illinois at Springfield), Nathalie Kuroiwa-Lewis (Saint Martin's University), Jennifer Smith Lapointe (Roberts Wesleyan College), Lezlie Knox (Marquette University), John R. Goss III (Shenandoah University), and Stephanie Chalupka (Worcester State University). I particularly enjoyed one reviewer's kind note stating, "*My students consistently tell me they enjoy the informal and emotional tone of Peter Elbow in his* Writing With Power, *and I am pleased to see that your book is just as friendly in its tone and style.*" These words warmed my heart and made me smile. It's not often that reviewers' words can do that.

Last, a BIG thank you to my father, Rev. Curtis C. Goodson, for having read every single word of the manuscript's drafts, for always offering sage advice, for editing so graciously, and for cheering me on when I got tired (which made for *a lot* of cheering!). No doubt about it, he deserves a raise! Maybe next time . . .

About the Author

Patricia Goodson is professor of health education in the Department of Health & Kinesiology at Texas A&M University (TAMU). She obtained a bachelor's degree in linguistics (from Universidade Estadual de Campinas) and a master's in philosophy of education (from Pontifícia Universidade Católica de Campinas) in Brazil; a master's in general theological studies (from Covenant Theological Seminary) and a PhD in health education (from the University of Texas at Austin) in the United States. At TAMU, she has taught mostly graduate-level courses such as Health Behavior Theory, Health Research Methods, Health Program Evaluation, Health Education Ethics, and Advanced Health Behavior Theory. In 2007, while acting as associate dean for Graduate Program Development, she created and implemented a college-wide writing support service for graduate students, based on the POWER model described in this book. Currently, as director of the College of Education and Human Development's Writing Initiative (POWER Services), she regularly offers Basic and Advanced Writing Studios for graduate students in the college and occasionally teaches writing workshops for faculty at Texas A&M and other universities. Dr. Goodson has won several department-, college-, and university-level awards for her teaching and research and was recently nominated by her colleagues for a faculty mentoring award. While she considers mentoring graduate students the most fulfilling part of her career, a couple of research interests vie for her attention. Her research focuses on topics such as sexual health of adults and adolescents and public health genomics. She has published extensively in high-impact journals, has reviewed for several prestigious publications, and has served as book review editor for *The Journal of Sex Research*. One of her intellectual passions is theory, and her previous book presents a critique of health education's current use of theory in both research and practice.

What you want is practice, practice, practice. It doesn't matter what we write . . . so long as we write continually as well as we can. I feel that every time I write a page either of prose or of verse, with real effort, even if it's thrown into the fire the next minute, I am so much further on.

—C. S. Lewis

Chapter One

Get Ready to Practice

Summary

The POWER Model

The Theory Behind POWER

The Research Behind POWER

Talent Development and Elite Performance: The Psychology Literature

Talent Development and Elite Performance: The Neuroscience Literature

Practicing Academic Writing

The style of an author should be the image of his mind, but the choice and command of language is the fruit of exercise.

Edward Gibbon (1737–1794)[1]

Wishing you could tackle all your writing assignments way ahead of deadline but wondering if this is even *possible*? Feeling as though you should be writing and publishing *more* but just don't know how to make it happen? Being pressured to write for publication in order to get promoted or tenured but unsure whether there will be enough time to get things out before you have to submit your packet? Having to write that thesis or dissertation but not envisioning how to tackle such a monstrous project? Feeling motivated but lost when piecing together a journal article for publication or a grant proposal for extramural funding?

Well . . . you're not alone.

Although writing and publishing define much of our lives as academics (professors, students, research staff, administrators), survey data show many faculty in U.S. colleges and universities publish less than one article or book per year (Belcher, 2009). What's more, within specific fields of inquiry such as social work, faculty members from 20% of the doctoral-granting programs are responsible for 43% of all journal articles published in that field (Green, Bellin, & Baskind, 2002). In other words, only a small number of college or university professors (in the United States and worldwide) write and publish at a steady, productive pace (Teodorescu, 2000).

When probed for reasons why they aren't writing or publishing more, both faculty and graduate students point to multiple barriers. Lack of time is the most common (DeAngelo, Hurtado, Pryor, Kelly, & Santos, 2009; Page-Adams, Cheng, Gogineni, Sruna, & Ching, 1995). Faculty and students claim they have difficulty fitting large chunks of writing time into their extremely busy schedules. And because many academics struggle with writing or lack confidence in their abilities, they relegate the task to the proverbial back burner.

As they (or should I say *we?*) systematically postpone a task they experience as difficult and unenjoyable, finding time to write, to start, or to complete a project looms over their academic lives like a guillotine, ready to plunge at any second (Steel, 2011). This is how writing controls our lives: through fear, avoidance, and stress. The more we avoid it, the more it controls us.

If you are such a writer—the kind who begins writing shortly before a deadline, who *knows* you should be writing but just can't feel motivated or find the time to do it, who isn't quite sure how to put together a publishable piece of academic writing—this book is for you. It will help you gain (or regain) control over your writing and disarm forever the guillotine of anxiety, fear, and stress.

The POWER Model

This book describes a model for taking control of the academic writing process—the POWER model (Promoting Outstanding Writing for Excellence in Research)—and provides weekly exercises to improve control. The model combines certain behavioral *principles* with specific *practices* to help you master and become comfortable with your writing. If you understand the principles and practice the exercises on a weekly basis, you will

    a. establish a *stress-free writing habit* that will serve you throughout your academic career;

    b. *increase your writing (and publishing) productivity* at a comfortable, consistent pace; and

    c. *improve the quality* of your academic writing (in two words: *write better*).

POWER embodies two related elements: (a) a writing support service created for faculty and graduate students in the College of Education and Human Development at Texas A&M University and (b) a set of principles and practices for promoting academic writing productivity and quality (in other words, a writing *model*).

POWER Services[2] are based on the POWER model. The model represents my effort to organize available theory and research data into useful strategies anyone can use. Peter Elbow (1998), Robert Boice (1990), Joseph Moxley and Todd Taylor (1997), along with Michael Mayrath (2008), are a few of the scholars who developed the theory and conducted the research supporting these strategies. Moreover, the neuroscience and psychology literature regarding the characteristics of elite performers, such as Olympic athletes, chess champions, and expert musicians, also anchor the exercises and suggestions contained in the model.

The Theory Behind POWER

The POWER model is grounded in Peter Elbow's (1998) theory of the writing process. Elbow refers to the notion of *writing with power* as encompassing two meanings. The first meaning alludes to powerful texts—the writing we see in poetry, religious documents, and political manifestos—the kind of writing that touches people's hearts, moves their souls, and fills them with courage (Rosenblatt, 2011).

Yet, anchoring this book is the *other* meaning in the phrase "writing with power": the idea that the writer has control and power over his/her writing. Writing with power, as Elbow (1998) defined it, "means getting *power over yourself and over the writing process:* knowing what you are doing as you write; being in charge; having control; not feeling stuck or helpless or intimidated" (p. viii; emphasis added).

Peter Elbow's theoretical approach to writing—in other words, his explanation for how good writing takes place (Goodson, 2010)—begins with the need to write badly, develops through the importance of sharing both early and late drafts, and results in gaining mastery over the writing, with the entire process becoming more pleasurable over time. According to Elbow (1998), when writers are comfortable generating initially messy texts, are eager to hear readers' reactions to what they wrote, and are motivated to rewrite their text to incorporate these reactions, only *then* will they begin to enjoy the writing process and the power it engenders. In his words,

> Once people have the feel of producing *some* words that were a pleasure to write and that make a dent on readers, they do better at putting in the enormous work needed to produce more of them. For really, the central question in writing (as with any difficult skill) is this: How can I get myself to put in the daunting time and effort I need for more consistent good results? The answer, I think, is to cheat—to look for pleasure and shortcuts. (p. xxi)

The POWER model and the exercises in this book, then, build on this theoretical perspective, emphasizing the value of initially messy writing, the need for practice, and the importance of feedback. If the principles, as well as each of the 50 exercises, are put into practice, they will nudge you into developing consistent and healthy writing habits, becoming more productive in your writing/publishing, and gaining power over your writing. Along the way, you may even surprise yourself by finding the entire process a bit more pleasant!

The Research Behind POWER

Much of the available data on faculty productivity were collected in the 1980s and 1990s. Despite being rather dated by now, the research remains valid because little has changed over time. Similar to the data I quoted regarding faculty in social work doctoral programs, data from faculty in science reveal that between 10% and 15% of authors are responsible for publishing 50% of everything read and cited in the field (Cole, 1981). Bolstering these dated findings, more recent surveys continue to indicate—as I mentioned earlier—that most professors in U.S. colleges and universities publish less than one article or book per year (Belcher, 2009).

What explains such low publication rates? Researchers such as Robert Boice (1989, 1990, 1997; Boice & Johnson, 1984), Joseph Moxley and Todd Taylor (1997), among others, examined academic writers' low productivity systematically. What they found pointed to faculty who struggled with getting their writing done and did not wish, or did not know how, to ask for help. Robert Boice (1990) wrote:

> In my two decades of experience with professors as writers, I've consistently seen people whose inexperience in discussing their blocks exceeded their shyness for revealing almost anything else, even sexual dysfunctions. They often came for help believing themselves to be unique as problem writers. And they worried that asking for help was an admission of weakness. (p. 1)

Research Shows . . .

Gerardo Ramirez and Sian L. Beilock (2011) tested whether a 10-minute expressive writing session before a high-stakes academic exam could prevent college and high school students' low performance due to test anxiety. The authors conducted four studies based on two important premises: (a) When people perform under pressure, their worries and anxiety about performance "compete for the working memory (WM) available for performance" (p. 211), leading to less optimal performance levels, and (b) expressive writing has been proven effective in dealing with traumatic or emotional experiences and therefore useful for regulating worry and anxiety.

Based on the studies' findings, the authors conclude that the expressive writing intervention "significantly improved students' exam scores, especially for students habitually anxious about test taking" (p. 211).

And they add, "For those students who are most anxious about success, one short writing intervention that brings testing pressures to the forefront enhances the likelihood of excelling, rather than failing, under pressure" (p. 213).

Dedicated to understanding and providing solutions for these professors, Boice and other scholars dug deep into academic writers' psyches and work habits. They found many explanations for academic writers' low productivity, including their strong critical sense or censorship, fears of failing, strong tendencies to perfectionism, struggles with procrastination, and negative writing experiences in the past. Poor mental/emotional health, personality type, work habits, attitudes toward writing, and perceptions of busyness were also identified as culprits for low writing productivity among faculty (Boice, 1989, 1990).

While psychologists such as Boice and Moxley zoomed in on individual-level factors, sociologists examined the problem of faculty productivity using a wide-angle lens. The broad image revealed multiple-level influences, including the socialization process faculty undergo when entering a professional field, the reinforcement and reward systems offered to them, as well as the quality of the academic training received during their doctoral programs (Neumann & Finaly-Neumann, 1990).

Even though sociologists identified structural elements that significantly impact academic writing productivity, it fell to psychologists to offer solutions to the problem. So far, at a broader, systemic level, little has been done to change the socialization process or the reward systems in which academics operate. Meanwhile, focusing on individual-level factors, psychologists devised specific strategies that professors and graduate students can adopt to improve their writing productivity.

The principles and practices you will find in this book are grounded in that psychology literature. The strategies include making writing a priority within one's daily schedule, managing distractions, and changing nonproductive attitudes toward writing (Moxley & Taylor, 1997). This book will also teach you the importance of obtaining feedback and establishing a social support system for yourself and your writing. I admit this with sadness, but the exercises will do nothing to change the structure of academic settings and how they reward writing. Perhaps *you* might take on this particular challenge?

While I anchor this book's principles and practices in the research on faculty productivity, two other bodies of knowledge also support the POWER model: (a) the psychology literature regarding elite performers and talent development and (b) the neuroscience literature focusing on the neurological dimension of extraordinary achievements, talent, and performance.

Talent Development and Elite Performance: The Psychology Literature

The work developed by K. Anders Ericsson represents a portion of the psychology literature regarding elite performance (Ericsson, Nandagopal, & Roring, 2009). Ericsson has done extensive research and theoretical development regarding elite performers' characteristics. With his observations, experiments, and theoretical reasoning, he has contributed to the scientific debate surrounding the question, "Is expert performance the result of innate talent (or genes), or of learned behavior (or practice)?"

Ericsson's (2007) conclusions point to the role of *deliberate practice* (sometimes also referred to as *deep practice*) as one vital element shaping expert performance:

> My central thesis is that experts continually engage in *deliberate practice* activities . . . that lead to refinement and maintenance of the mediating mechanisms [such as mental representation, anticipation skills, and control of motor actions, among others]. In contrast, less-accomplished individuals

do not engage in these activities once they have reached an acceptable level. Their performance is prematurely arrested in its effortless automated form. (p. 12)

Put simply, Ericsson's thesis is this: Elite performers differ from non-elite performers in one key element—*deliberate practice*. Non-elite performers will learn a certain task—playing golf, for example—and will practice just enough to become "competent players." Once they feel they've achieved a satisfactory level, they stop practicing. Elite performers, on the other hand, don't stop. Instead, they sustain practice in order to maintain and further refine the basic skills they achieved (see also Colvin, 2010, for more on deep practice).

Talent Development and Elite Performance: The Neuroscience Literature

Curiously, neuroscientists researching expert performers have come to the same conclusions about practice as those reached by psychologists: Deep practice or deliberate practice is one (if not *the one*) key element for developing extraordinary skills. In *The Talent Code*, Daniel Coyle (2009) proposes to find answers to the question, "What explains exceptional talent?" Not surprisingly, one of the first answers he unveils is *deep practice*, and he offers this insight:

Deep practice is built on a paradox: struggling in certain targeted ways—operating at the edges of your ability, where you make mistakes—makes you smarter. Or to put it a slightly different way, experiences where you're forced to slow down, make errors, and correct them—as you would if you were walking up an ice-covered hill, slipping and stumbling as you go—end up making you swift and graceful without your realizing it. (p. 18)

Yet Coyle uncovered that practice, by itself, does not explain talent or expert performance. It's what happens to our brains *during* or as a *result of* deep practice that accounts for the expertise.

Coyle (2009) begins describing the importance of what happens during and after practice by first admitting the biases he brought to his investigation. Similar to what most of us understand about how human brains work, Coyle believed the most important element or portion of our brains was the neuron network. But while interviewing numerous neuroscientists to learn about expert talent and performance from their points of view, Coyle learned these neuroscientists were experiencing an important shift in their thinking: As important as the neurons and their synapses are for brain function, it appears that *myelin*—the substance insulating the nerve wires in our brains—might have an even more prominent role than the neurons themselves. Coyle describes this shift in thinking as a "Copernican-size revolution" and adds:

> The revolution is built on three simple facts: (1) Every human movement, thought, or feeling is a precisely timed electrical signal traveling through a chain of neurons—a circuit of nerve fibers. (2) Myelin is the insulation that wraps these nerve fibers and increases signal strength, speed, and accuracy. (3) The more we fire a particular circuit, the more myelin optimizes that circuit, and the stronger, faster, and more fluent our movements and thoughts become. (p. 32)

Practice allows us to fire specific circuits in our brains repeatedly and to develop more myelin. In turn, more myelin leads to faster or more optimal firing of circuits and developing of skills, as explained in this exchange between Coyle (2009) and the neuroscientist George Bartzokis:

> "What do good athletes do when they train?" Bartzokis said. "They send precise impulses along wires that give the signal to myelinate that wire. They end up, after all the training, with a super-duper wire—lots of bandwidth, a high-speed T-3 line. That's what makes them different from the rest of us." (pp. 32–33)

As Coyle (2009) recounts in his book, nearly all extraordinary talent can be explained by tremendous amounts of practice and consequent myelin production. One example he gives relates specifically to writing: the Brontë sisters, Charlotte, Emily, and Anne. Many literary scholars have labeled them "natural-born novelists" and poets because they wrote prolifically at very young ages (p. 56). Yet the facts suggest that instead of being naturally talented they were born into a literary-nurturing environment, engaged in a significant amount of practice very early in their lives, and produced quite a lot of poor (yes: *poor!*) writing early on. Coyle writes,

> Deep practice and myelin [as opposed to "natural talent"] give us a better way to look at the Brontës. The unskilled quality of their early writing isn't a contradiction of the literary heights they eventually achieved—it's a prerequisite to it. They became great writers not *in spite of* the fact that they started out immature and imitative but *because* they were willing to spend vast amounts of time and energy being immature and imitative, building myelin in the confined, safe space of their little books. Their childhood writings were collaborative deep practice, where they developed storytelling muscles. (p. 57)

Granted, both the psychology and neuroscience literature also list several other factors, alongside myelin, as playing roles in developing above-ordinary talent. These factors include exposure to skilled mentoring/teaching and skill acquisition at young ages. Yet the central, common element in all the research is *practice,* with its consequent *myelin building.*

Practicing Academic Writing

So, what does all this mean for us academics? What does it mean for our writing productivity and writing quality? Simply put, it means this: If we commit to *practice our academic writing*—and obtain continual feedback—our writing and productivity levels will improve!

And how can we *practice* academic writing, besides by just . . . well, just *writing?* We can incorporate practice exercises designed to develop specific dimensions of our writing, much as we would do if we were attempting to strengthen and build specific muscles in our bodies through physical exercise. This book will provide the opportunity to *practice* your writing on a regular basis. It is designed to give you a chance to repeat an exercise, make mistakes, correct them, and, with repetition and feedback, add to the myelin you already have and improve. As Ronald T. Kellogg and Alison P. Whiteford (2009) state in "Training Advanced Writing Skills: The Case for Deliberate Practice":

> The term *deliberate practice* refers to practice undertaken with a specific goal to improve. The learner mindfully engages in practice designed by an instructor, coach, mentor, or tutor, who further provides corrective feedback as encouragement to excel. (p. 251)

Please note that—as the quote above emphasizes—an important element in this practice approach involves *obtaining feedback* so we can correct our mistakes and incorporate the corrections when rewriting. Therefore, you may want first to take a close look at Chapter 2 (where we practice creating a writing habit) and Chapter 5 (where we practice securing support and feedback). Making sure we develop a system for continually obtaining feedback will help our practice significantly.

I hope this brief incursion into psychology and neuroscience helps you see how this book is grounded in both a theoretical and an empirical platform. I also hope that the evidence pointing to the value of gaining control over your writing, the importance of deliberate practice (with feedback), and the contributions a text such as this one can make to the process will motivate you even more to plunge into these exercises and improve your writing productivity.

Notes

1. Quotations heading each of the chapters were chosen from a selection culled by Gregory Victor Babic (2008) and published in *Words to Inspire Writers*. All quotations are in the public domain.

2. A graduate student at Texas A&M University can go to http://power.tamu .edu to schedule an appointment with a consultant (or with me), to obtain feedback and support while working on a writing project. If you are at another university, you may want to consider creating a service such as POWER for the graduate students at your school.

Electronic Sources

Texas A&M University Writing Support Services: http://power.tamu.edu

References

Babic, G. V. (2008). *Words to inspire writers*. Australia: F. C. Sach.

Belcher, W. L. (2009). *Writing your journal article in 12 weeks: A guide to academic publishing success*. Thousand Oaks, CA: Sage.

Boice, R. (1989). Procrastination, busyness and bingeing. *Behaviour Research and Therapy, 27*(6), 605–611.

Boice, R. (1990). *Professors as writers: A self-help guide to productive writing*. Stillwater, OK: New Forums Press.

Boice, R. (1997). Which is more productive, writing in binge patterns of creative illness or in moderation? *Written Communication, 14*(4), 435–459.

Boice, R., & Johnson, K. (1984). Perception and practice of writing for publication by faculty at a doctoral-granting university. *Research in Higher Education, 21,* 33–45.

Cole, J. R. (1981). Women in science. *American Scientist, 69,* 385–391.

Colvin, G. (2010). *Talent is overrated: What really separates world-class performers from everybody else*. New York: Portfolio (Penguin Group).

Coyle, D. (2009). *The talent code: Greatness isn't born. It's grown. Here's how.* New York: Bantam Dell.

DeAngelo, L., Hurtado, S., Pryor, J. H., Kelly, K. R., & Santos, J. L. (2009). *The American college teacher: National norms for the 2007–2008 HERI faculty survey*. Los Angeles: Higher Education Research Institute, UCLA.

Elbow, P. (1998). *Writing with power: Techniques for mastering the writing process* (2nd ed.). New York: Oxford University Press.

Ericsson, K. A. (2007). Deliberate practice and the modifiability of body and mind: Toward a science of the structure and acquisition of expert and elite performance. *International Journal of Sport Psychology, 38,* 4–34.

Ericsson, K. A., Nandagopal, K., & Roring, R. W. (2009). Toward a science of exceptional achievement: Attaining superior performance through deliberate practice. *Longevity, Regeneration, and Optimal Health: Ann. N.Y. Acad. Sci., 1172,* 199–217.

Goodson, P. (2010). *Theory in health promotion research and practice: Thinking outside the box.* Sudbury, MA: Jones & Bartlett.

Green, R. G., Bellin, M. H., & Baskind, F. R. (2002). Results of the doctoral faculty publication project: Journal article productivity and its correlates in the 1990s. *Journal of Social Work Education, 38*(1), 135–152.

Kellogg, R. T., & Whiteford, A. P. (2009). Training advanced writing skills: The case for deliberate practice. *Educational Psychologist, 44*(4), 250–266.

Mayrath, M. (2008). Attributions of productive authors in educational psychology journals. *Educational Psychology Review, 20,* 41–56.

Moxley, J. M., & Taylor, T. (Eds.). (1997). *Writing and publishing for academic authors* (2nd ed.). Lanham, MD: Rowman & Littlefield.

Neumann, Y., & Finaly-Neumann, E. (1990). The support-stress paradigm and faculty research publication. *Journal of Higher Education, 61*(5), 565–580.

Page-Adams, D., Cheng, L. C., Gogineni, A., Sruna, S., & Ching, Y. (1995). Establishing a group to encourage writing for publication among doctoral students. *Journal of Social Work Education, 31*(3), 402–407.

Ramirez, G., & Beilock, S. L. (2011). Writing about testing worries boosts exam performance in the classroom. *SCIENCE, 331*(14), 211–213.

Rosenblatt, R. (2011). *Unless it moves the human heart: The craft and art of writing.* New York: HarperCollins.

Steel, P. (2011). *The procrastination equation: How to stop putting things off and start getting stuff done.* New York: Harper.

Teodorescu, D. (2000). Correlates of faculty publication productivity: A cross-national analysis. *Higher Education, 39,* 201–222.

Part I

Practice Becoming a Productive Academic Writer

Chapter Two

Establish and Maintain the "Write" Habit

Summary

Think About It . . .

Seeing Yourself as a Writer

   STEP 1: Embrace the "Write" Attitude

   STEP 2: Manage the Contingencies

   STEP 3: Practice

EXERCISE 1—Schedule Your Writing Sessions

EXERCISE 2—Increase Your Writing Time in No Time

EXERCISE 3—Write Quickly, Edit Slowly

EXERCISE 4—Organize Messy Drafts

EXERCISE 5—Keep and Share a Writing Log

EXERCISE 6—Read About Writing

EXERCISE 7—Document Your Writing Projects

EXERCISE 8—Write to Learn (Anything, Including How to Write)

We are what we repeatedly do.

Excellence, then, is not an act, but a habit.

Aristotle (384–322 B.C.)

Think About It . . .

If I asked you to complete this sentence, what would you say?

The most important tool for success as an academic is _____.

When I invite students in my classes to go through this sentence-completion exercise, they quickly come up with "critical thinking," "research skills," or "statistics" as their answer. Because they are in a writing productivity class, however, they suspect I'm going to say something like "writing," so some volunteer answers such as "publications" or "articles published in professional journals." But rarely do they point to *writing,* itself, as the most important tool.

I'm not sure why they don't come up with *writing* as their answer. Do they believe that writing is a by-product of research or teaching? That writing is merely a necessary evil, something one "gets to" only when there's an assignment to complete, if there's enough spare time? That what matters most are the completed papers, the published products, not the process itself?

I also ask graduate students and faculty who attend my workshops to share how they reply to the question, "What do you do for a living?" I probe to see how many will say, "I am a writer; I write for a living." Curiously, few, if any, ever identify themselves as professional writers.

With these two reflexive exercises, I come to my point, to the single take-home message I want them to remember if they happen to learn nothing else in my classes or workshops: *They are writers.* They write for a living. Every dimension of their future success as academics—grades, promotions, presentations to professional groups, funding for research projects—will depend on how well (and, yes, *how much*) they write. Aside from trade book authors, no other professional group depends so strongly on writing for its survival. Academics (here, I'm thinking of faculty, students, research staff, and even administrators) are professional writers, whether they identify themselves as such or not, whether they like it or not.

Therefore, the single most important take-home message I want *you* to remember is this: **You are a professional writer.** If you are a college student, a graduate student, faculty, research staff, or an administrator, you write for a living. You may not make as much money from book sales as modern-day authors such as Stephen King, Michael Crichton, or Patricia Cornwell make. After all, these authors have published at least one best seller a year, over many years, in the United States. Yet, as it happens with these famous authors, your salary and your success will largely depend on how much and how well you write. No doubt about it, **academics write for a living.** Therefore, *you* write for a living, whether you like it or not, whether you want to or not.

Writing term papers, reports, reviews, journal articles, book chapters, research grants, books, or textbooks defines much of students' and faculty's lives in colleges and universities worldwide. Yet as you read in Chapter 1, research data suggest faculty write and publish at lower-than-expected levels, while students struggle to respond to their professors' expectations for their writing.

In part, the low productivity and struggles with writing have to do with how academics view themselves and their work. If they do not see themselves as *writers,* their writing becomes relegated to whenever they have *enough time.* Enough time never happens spontaneously, so they seldom write. Even though writing represents THE most important tool in the academician's toolbox for professional advancement, we (yes, I, too, have been guilty of this) treat it much as we do our gardening tools: shoved to the back of the toolshed or garage, stored among the other dusty, rusty tools, and used only sporadically, when absolutely necessary. As many of you who love to have the right tool for the right job already know, certain equipment—when used infrequently—deteriorates and loses its efficiency.

Seeing Yourself as a Writer

The exercises in this book, therefore, were designed to help you develop *a new perspective of yourself as a writer.* A new perspective will help you view your work in a new light and, consequently, improve your productivity with minimal struggle. But to develop this new perspective, you'll need to take three steps:

STEP 1: Embrace the "write" attitude.

STEP 2: Manage the contingencies.

STEP 3: Practice.

STEP 1: Embrace the "Write" Attitude

The first action step you must take to develop a healthy and sustainable writing habit is to adopt the appropriate or right attitude.

What is an attitude, then? And which attitude is the most appropriate? In psychology, the simplest definition of attitude regards it as the judgment human beings make of everything around them (their environment, other people, situations, and themselves) as good or bad, favorable or unfavorable, positive or negative, pleasurable or displeasing, likeable or unlikable (Albarracin, Johnson, & Zanna, 2005, p. 3).

While scholars disagree about how many dimensions an attitude has, for our purposes we'll adopt the simplest construction: an attitude comprises two important dimensions—a belief and a value. The formula is straightforward: A strong, favorable belief, combined with a high value, produces a strong, positive attitude. Put simply, if you believe developing a healthy, sustainable, stress-free writing habit will lead to better-quality writing and more steady production, then you have a positive belief about developing a writing habit. If writing well and producing more steadily without stress are important to you, then what you believe in has a high value. When combined—the belief together with the value—they form an attitude. When the belief is positive and the value is high, the attitude is strong and favorable. When the belief is negative and the value is low, you have a negative attitude.

The most appropriate and helpful attitude you can embrace as an academic writer is this one: (a) *believing* that developing a healthy writing habit CAN, in fact, lead to improvements in the quality of your writing and to stress-free productivity AND (b) *valuing* improvement and stress-free productivity.

If you admit not having this attitude, right now . . . well, good for you! You're being honest, and honesty is very important for powerful academic writing. But don't lose heart. Attitudes take time to develop, as they are influenced or shaped by everyday experience, practice, and reinforcement. Therefore, if you don't have a positive attitude this very minute, I invite you to follow along with the book and see if your attitude improves. The exercises I propose in the text are designed to shape your writing experience positively, to provide opportunities for practice, and to facilitate obtaining reinforcement. Engaging in these practices will help you develop a more favorable attitude toward writing and help you see yourself as a professional writer. If you do, however, have a positive attitude right now, then you're already on the road to better writing and increased productivity! Welcome!

STEP 2: Manage the Contingencies

Embracing the "write" attitude, however, is only the first step you need to take to establish and sustain a healthy writing habit. The research on academics' writing productivity points to the need for *managing contingencies,* too (Boice, 1983, 1997b). Managing contingencies means handling and controlling the factors that either facilitate or hinder your ability to write regularly.

Contingencies are the circumstances and events surrounding you, which affect your writing habit. For example, checking your e-mail or Facebook page is a contingency (Carr, 2011). If you check them too frequently, this may distract you from getting any writing done. By scheduling a specific writing time in your schedule/planner and turning off your e-mail or Internet access, you will be managing an important distraction. You will be paying attention exclusively to the writing during your writing sessions, distraction-free. You will be managing some of your contingencies.

Research Shows . . .

Robert Boice (1997a) studied a sample of 40 "blocked" academic writers and what they said to themselves while writing. When examining the self-talk data, Boice observed that 74% of what blocked writers said to themselves while writing was maladaptive, or not helpful. Only 7% of their self-talk "could be construed as helpful." Here is a list of the most common maladaptive thoughts exhibited by this sample:

1. Writing is too fatiguing and unpleasant; almost anything else would be more fun.
2. It's O.K. to put writing off, to procrastinate.
3. I'm not in the mood to write; I'm too depressed or unmotivated to write.
4. I feel impatient about writing; I need to rush to catch up on all the projects that I should already have finished.
5. My writing must be mistake-free and better than the usual stuff that gets published.
6. My writing will probably be criticized and I may feel humiliated.
7. Good writing is done in a single draft, preferably in a long session. (p. 30)

STEP 3: Practice

In addition to adopting a favorable attitude and managing your contingencies, you will need to take one last step: Practice your writing. The research done on musicians and athletes suggests the most important element distinguishing elite performers from mediocre ones is the time spent on *deliberate* (or *deep*) *practice.* (For some interesting descriptions of deep practice, see Daniel Coyle's [2009] *The Talent Code,* Geoff Colvin's [2010] *Talent Is Overrated,* and K. Anders Ericsson's [2007, 2008; Ericsson, Nandagopal, & Roring, 2009] research, mentioned in Chapter 1.) Deliberate practice means targeted, focused repetition of specific behaviors—accompanied by persistent correcting of mistakes—for the purpose of improving performance (again, see Chapter 1 for more on *deep* or *deliberate practice;* see also Cleary & Zimmerman, 2001; Kitsantas & Zimmerman, 2006; and Zimmerman & Kitsantas, 1999).

The key to optimizing *deep practice* is to s-l-o-w d-o-w-n during practice. Slowing down forces the one practicing to pay attention to mistakes, identify them, and correct them immediately. The exercises in this book are designed to help you practice writing by slowing down, paying attention to your unique patterns of mistakes, and developing a system for getting feedback to correct those mistakes.

Contrary to popular belief, *practicing our writing* requires more than sitting down and "just doing it," just writing, writing, writing. Practice entails repeating an action with a defined purpose, a specific strategy, and a mechanism for correcting mistakes. Practice—especially deep practice—entails more than mere repetition. Deep practice involves slowing down, paying attention to mistakes, and correcting them as soon as possible. The exercises in this book will help you precisely with slowing down, with strategizing repetitions, as well as with catching and correcting mistakes.

Rarely do we think about approaching our academic writing from a perspective of *practice.* When was the last time someone told you they couldn't meet with you because they had a writing practice session scheduled for that time? As you work through this book you will learn to respect and protect your writing time much as Olympian athletes protect their practice schedules.

This book is anchored, therefore, in the well-established reputation of deep practice for expert performance in many areas, and it will attempt to shift your attitude to one that values *practicing your writing* (see Chapter 1 for further details on the empirical and theoretical basis grounding this notion). In sum, the exercises I propose were designed to help you *develop the "write" attitude, manage your contingencies,* and *practice your writing.* Let's begin!

EXERCISE 1—SCHEDULE YOUR WRITING SESSIONS

TIME NEEDED: 15 minutes in the first session; 05 minutes thereafter

MATERIALS NEEDED: Your weekly/daily planner; a timer

This week's exercise will establish the foundation for all other exercises in the book. Scheduling your writing sessions is the single best contingency-management strategy you can adopt. Research examining productive faculty's habits consistently points to scheduled and protected writing time as a key element for success. One example is the study Michael C. Mayrath (2008) conducted with 22 of the most productive faculty in educational psychology. The question posed to the faculty was, "If you were going to explain why you were so productive, what would you say?" (p. 46). Among the answers participants gave, "scheduled time to write" emerged prominently:

> Karen Harris [one of the participants in the study] said she was taught a "calendar trick by a very productive researcher" when she was an assistant professor. The trick is that "research and writing time belong on your calendar." She said an author must write in [the calendar] time to write and do research, and that you must protect this time just as if it were a meeting that you could not reschedule. (p. 52)

If the strategy is essential for extremely successful scholars, why wouldn't it be helpful for us, too? Therefore, take 10 minutes, right now, and examine your weekly/daily planner. Then, do the following:

1. Schedule your writing sessions for this week. Schedule one session *every day*. Yes! Every day! (I recommend at least 1 day off per week, however). And, if your schedule allows: schedule each session at the *same time* every day (try your best to make this happen).

2. Start with **15-minute sessions** if you're not used to writing regularly. Plan for 30-minute sessions if you're more used to writing routinely. I am certain you can find a block of 15 minutes, every day, somewhere in your busy schedule.

3. After scheduling the days/times you will be writing this week, spend the remaining 5 minutes listing what pops into your head when I ask you the question highlighted below (just write a bulleted list, as the ideas come to mind). Write as quickly as you can. Don't worry about editing or capturing your thoughts in complete sentences; single words will do:

   - What does it take to get me to write (to begin and/or to continue)?

4. In each writing session this week, use 5 of your scheduled 15 minutes (or 30 minutes) to answer these other questions (one question per writing session):

   a. What keeps me away from writing?
   b. What aspects of writing do I really enjoy?
   c. What aspects of writing do I especially dislike?
   d. How have I been treating my most important academic tool? Is it rusting away, out of reach or sight, needing repair, polishing, sharpening? Or is it always right here, in a clean, airy place, fully functional and ready when I need it? In other words, how much time and resources have I dedicated lately to improving my writing?

After you've done Exercise 1, keep your writing schedule for this week. During each session, however, write (or don't write) as you normally would. If you feel you have nothing to write about, read a journal article and note your thoughts as you write. If you're really having difficulty figuring out what to write, practice copying a text—yes, copying (more on the benefits of copying in Exercise 15). Or write about your experiences with developing a writing habit, or write a letter. I doubt—because you're an academic—you will struggle to find *something* to write about. This week, the purpose is to begin developing a writing habit; the goal, to get used to showing up for your writing sessions. *What* you write about right now is not as important as training your body and your mind to follow a specific routine, to create a writing habit. Remember: Athletes, musicians, and other world-class performers spend much of their time in practice sessions. Regularly. Consistently. Why shouldn't *you?*

After the first week, revisit your planned schedule and make any necessary changes. Eventually, you will learn which time slots work best for you, depending on your routine and your demands.

Being an academic myself, I realize you may be asking, "But when will I find time to practice writing within my already packed schedule?" Once, when I was asking the same question, I came across this brilliant quote in Johnson and Mullen's (2007) *Write to the Top!*:

> Prolific academics *create* writing time ***where none exists*** and then carefully *protect* it from intrusion. (p. 8; emphasis added)

Notice the difference here? *Create* versus *find*. None of us can ever find time because we look for *extra* time—those minutes left over, unclaimed, after everything else is cared for. Such time rarely, if ever, can be found! Yet all of us can purposefully *create* and *protect* time to write. I suggest you print the quote above and post it next to your workstation as a reminder of what you're practicing this week. Try it. It works!

EXERCISE 2—INCREASE YOUR WRITING TIME IN NO TIME

TIME NEEDED: 05 minutes x session

MATERIALS NEEDED: Timer

In Exercise 2, you will be adding 1 minute of writing time to your regular writing sessions, one session at a time, like this:

Session 1: your regular writing time + 1 minute

Session 2: your regular writing time + 2 minutes

Session 3: your regular writing time + 3 minutes

And so on.

The goal is to increase the time you spend on your scheduled writing sessions by 50% to 100%. If you began with 15 minutes, you'll build up to 30 minutes in 15 days; if you began with 30 minutes, you'll build up to 45 minutes. For this to happen, you will need to continue adding 1 minute for at least 15 sessions. If you practice the exercise for 1 week only, you can add an average 5 minutes to your regular writing time. It's up to you how much you want to increase your writing time, overall.

After setting your timer for the extra minute, spend the first 5 minutes of each writing session during the week examining the lists you generated last week (Exercise 1). Identify three factors that facilitate your writing (that motivate you to start writing, make writing enjoyable for you, or keep you writing once you begin) and three factors that keep you away from writing.

This week, develop **one strategy** to handle each factor hindering your writing. For example, if you're always tempted to check your e-mail during a writing session, or if you feel you can't begin to write before you check your e-mail, try turning it off when you sit down to write. Allow yourself to check it only *after* you've completed your writing session for the day. Use the e-mail checking as a reward for having written that day.

Once you've developed three new strategies to deal with the obstacles to writing, focus on the factors that facilitate your writing: What's working really well? Can more of what's working be added to your writing routine? How can you make what's already working well even better?

Test your strategies, and adapt or modify them as needed. Make them work for you. In my case, avoiding interruptions while I write is very important. When I first began managing these interruptions, I tried closing my office door during my writing sessions and placing signs on the door asking people not to disturb me because I was writing: *"Interrupt at your own risk! I'm writing!"* I've now settled into arriving at my office early in the mornings, when no one is around to interrupt (I aim for 7:00 A.M., most days). How did I get used to arriving earlier at the office? By setting my alarm clock 1 minute earlier every day for a month. After a month, I was getting up half an hour before I used to, without even noticing the difference!

EXERCISE 3—WRITE QUICKLY, EDIT SLOWLY

TIME NEEDED: 10 minutes x session

MATERIALS NEEDED: Timer

This week's exercise will allow you to practice an important principle for productive writing: **separating the generating from the editing.** Generating a written text requires creativity and involves activating specific mechanisms in our brains. Editing text, on the other hand, is an analytical and repetitive action, requiring attention to detail. Editing invokes brain mechanisms distinct from those used in creative tasks. Our brain is an amazingly complex system, capable of handling myriad intricate jobs (Medina, 2008). Even so, it doesn't perform very well when trying to handle two tasks requiring focused attention, such as *generating* and *editing,* simultaneously (so much for the notion of multitasking!).

Many people complain of writer's block because they attempt to generate and edit at the same time. They want the first sentence they write to be *the perfect sentence!* And so they wait, and sit, and stare at their screens, hoping for the one perfect sentence to bubble up, somehow, from a fountain of wisdom buried deep, somewhere. It rarely—if ever—happens. They continue to wait, sit, and stare, sometimes for hours! Frustration then settles in; the belief *"I can't write!"* takes over. Peter Elbow (1998)—the writing theoretician I mentioned in Chapter 1—calls this "the dangerous method: trying to write it right the first time" (p. 39).

Writers who heed Elbow's warning and separate generating from editing fare much better. They write more and don't experience writer's block, compared with those who try to tackle both editing and generating at the same time. Therefore, the exercise for this week aims at having you practice separating generative writing (the capturing of words, thoughts, ideas) from editing.

So . . . begin by setting your timer for 5 minutes. For these first 5 minutes, write all the thoughts tumbling in your mind. The requirement, here, is the following: Write *as fast as you can,* without stopping. Don't allow your fingers to stop typing at any time; don't lift your pen/pencil from the writing pad at all for the entire 5 minutes.

If you write on a computer, you may want to minimize your file so you don't see what you are typing and don't feel tempted to backtrack in order to correct misspellings, change words, redo punctuation. These small tasks will derail your thoughts and cause you to microswitch between the two tasks, the generating and the editing. You want to avoid this, completely.

You may write about anything on your mind at the moment, or you may write all the thoughts you've been accumulating related to your current writing project. The principle, here, is to generate a lot of words by capturing all those random thoughts twirling around in your head. You don't want to stop and think about what to write; you want to write in order to *see* what's on your mind.

The rules, then, for the exercise are these: Write as fast as you can, capture as many loose thoughts as possible, and don't worry (or even think) about mistakes, appropriate language, spelling, grammar, punctuation. That's why it's highly recommended you don't see your words while you're generating them; you'll have plenty of time to look at them during the editing phase.

When your 5 minutes are up, STOP. Reset your alarm for another 5 minutes and focus on cleaning up the mess you just created. You might

- look for good ideas to develop or rescue from the mess,
- place all similar ideas together—like with like,
- organize the text (move sentences around to make more sense), or
- generate a few more sentences to complement what you have.

This is an exercise you should slowly transfer into your daily writing sessions. As you become more comfortable with it, plan for splitting your writing sessions into two more-or-less equal portions. Use the first portion to generate only then edit during the second period.

As your text matures, you'll be increasing the time spent editing while decreasing the time spent generating. But keep in mind the process is iterative, because editing will quite frequently require that you generate a few more words, rewrite a few sentences, or add connecting phrases.

A **variation on this exercise** you may want to try later, after you've practiced the one above for at least a week, is this: Instead of splitting each writing session into two portions (one for generating and one for editing), use various sessions only for generating, then several subsequent sessions only for editing. I know this method as the "fast writing, slow editing" process. It is described in an article written by Elena A. Mikhailova and Linda B. Nilson (2007) titled "Developing Prolific Scholars: The 'Fast Article Writing' Methodology."

Tip for ESL Writers

Try to generate your text in English (if you're writing for an English-speaking audience). As you write quickly, nonstop, however, you may not remember certain words or phrases in English. No problem: Write them in your native language. Later, during the editing phase, you can translate the text into English.

What is important? That you capture your thoughts and reasoning about the topic. It doesn't matter if, while you're capturing them, the text comes out garbled, messy, incoherent, grammatically incorrect, or in a mix of two or three languages! You can ALWAYS come back and clean up the messy text. But if you don't capture that idea you had a few minutes ago, it may be gone for a while or, worse, lost forever!

EXERCISE 4—ORGANIZE MESSY DRAFTS

TIME NEEDED: 10 minutes x session

MATERIALS NEEDED: Timer; the text you generated last week

Once you've generated a bunch of words—and it's important to have a bunch of words you can, in fact, throw away—it's time to see whether there are any ideas that can be salvaged from the rubble. Begin by focusing on a single page of messy writing. Work on one page per day as your exercise or deliberate practice for this week. Highlight—yes, with a pen, or with the highlighter in your word processor—one key idea you wish to keep. Copy and paste that highlighted idea into a new file. Return to the messy file and continue to read. Read each remaining sentence. Do any of those sentences contain an idea similar to the one you highlighted and pasted into the new file? If so, copy and paste it next to the first idea. This way, you begin to organize the ideas in your messy draft, much in the same way you would organize the silverware in your kitchen drawer: knives go with knives, spoons with spoons, forks with forks. Place like with like. Similar ideas together.

At this point it does not matter—at all—whether you have three sentences saying the same thing or whether they are well written or even connected in any way. All you are looking for are similar ideas: like with like. Proceed with the same strategy, one page at a time. Or, if you choose to, apply this strategy in your writing session today, after you have generated at least half a page of messy text. You may want to split your daily writing sessions in half and plan to generate (only) during the first half, then to organize like with like (only) during the second half.

Example

Consider the messy text I wrote as a first draft for a small research grant submitted in 2010. The grant proposal focused on testing the potential relationship between writing and exercising. Notice the notes to myself, the reminders, and the complete disregard for punctuation, grammar, or spelling. When I generated this text, I minimized the file on my computer screen so I wouldn't see what I typed. Try this strategy: It really frees you from wanting to go back and correct each little typing mistake you make!

Begin with: why should we care if there is a relationship between exercise and writing? We care because, if we find a relationship, we can make a case for keeping/increase physical activity in schools, and we can propose mechanisms that facilitate writing (productivity & quality) among academics. Why? Because many academics struggle with writing, despite perceptions of the contrary. Because little is being invested in training graduate students to become lifelong, academic writers in their fields. Because, ultimately, science, technology, and knowledge broadly speaking cannot advance without quality writing. Indirectly, even though we propose this study with a sample of college students, it may provide important clue for replication among younger school children, who are, themselves, learning to master the mechanic of cognitions involved in writing.

This study, then, has implication that might reach beyond the samples being studied, here.

(PAT: Need to define productivity). Here, we define writing productivity, as the production of writing products (publications or grant submissions) done at a regular pace, and consistently over time.

Need to also define physical exercise. (Ask P. for a general definition).

As I organized these messy ideas, like with like, I came up with the following:

Central Question: Why should we care if there is a relationship between exercise and writing?

Argument/Answer: We should care because: 1) findings will help build the case for keeping physical education in the schools' curricula; 2) findings may help develop tailored strategies for improving academic writing; and 3) because solutions to improve academic writing are needed.

Background: 1) academic writers struggle with writing; 2) science, technology, and knowledge-base in all fields require good writing in order to develop.

Implications: potential to transfer information from this study's sample to other populations (external validity).

Other ideas to develop: little is being done to enhance writing skills among graduate students.

Definitions Needed: writing productivity; physical exercise/physical activity.

Notice how—because I wrote the text (quickly, I might add)—I wasn't concerned about paragraph structure, or grammar, or organization. I aimed for capturing my initial thoughts about the project, as well as what the readers would want to see in the proposal. I also needed to note which constructs I would have to define clearly (both for the readers and for myself). When I went back to organize what I had, I saw a much clearer picture of what I needed to write: the arguments I needed to develop and strengthen with supporting data, the topic's background, the potential implications, as well as a few methodological matters I had to address.

In the end, here's how this text looked. Please note, it took several edits/ rewrites and feedback from my co-investigator to arrive at this final version.

Also note, I had several citations embedded in the segment, but I deleted them to make it easier for you to read:

> *Rationale*—Why should researchers care to explore the relationship between physical activity and academic writing? First, because this relationship has yet to be systematically examined, even though related studies have shown physical activity (especially aerobic exercise) can enhance school children's and adolescents' overall academic performance/achievement and improve cognitive functions in various age groups. Second, because if writing is the most important skill for success in academia, identifying strategies to promote healthy writing habits and improve writing productivity/quality should be a concern for university administrators, faculty, and graduate students. Given the established association among physical activity, academic performance/ achievement, and cognition, it is reasonable to assume that promoting physical activity may represent a viable strategy for enhancing graduate students' writing habits, productivity, and quality.
>
> *Purpose*—The purpose of this study, therefore, is to explore whether a relationship between physical exercise and improvement in writing habits, productivity & quality, among graduate students, occurs. If our data support this relationship, the subsequent step will consist of securing other funding sources to study the mechanisms underlying the relationship. This proposed study (and subsequent ones) can contribute significant knowledge and practical strategies to the interdisciplinary fields of neuroscience, education, and graduate student development.

Although this may not be an outstanding piece of writing, the text achieved its purpose: to communicate *what* we wanted to do in the project and *why*.

So spend 10 minutes on this exercise every day. Even if you don't complete a whole page organizing like with like, limit yourself to 10 minutes maximum and return to the exercise during your next writing session. Because this represents a *strategy*—more than merely a simple exercise—you will find yourself employing the technique repeatedly in your writing, and, with time, you will become proficient in organizing! You also will notice your initial messy drafts beginning to look less messy over time. You will amaze yourself!

EXERCISE 5—KEEP AND SHARE A WRITING LOG

TIME NEEDED: 05 minutes x session

MATERIALS NEEDED: Timer; a partner or writing buddy whom you trust

This week's exercise will have you practice keeping track of your writing time. You will create a writing log for yourself (or adapt the one available for download at www.sagepub.com/goodson). After you have created your log, you will practice BEGINNING and ENDING each writing session by entering data into your log.

When I teach this strategy in my classes or writing workshops, participants invariably ask the questions, "And how does this help? Sounds like more work, to me, having to write down my writing time . . . Is it really necessary?" I am the first to shun the idea of extra (especially useless) work. I already have too much work scheduled on my agenda; don't need any more, thank you very much. So I do understand students' concerns about keeping a writing log. In attempting to assuage their concerns, however, I share my own writing logs with them and tell them how keeping a log has fulfilled three important purposes in my writing life: (a) It has kept me on track and held me accountable to myself (when I say I spent 1 hour writing today, I have documentation that, in fact, I did spend 1 hour writing), (b) it has served as an important positive reinforcement at times when I didn't know where my time went during an especially busy week (it certainly didn't go into writing, did it?), and (c) it serves to hold me accountable to other people, such as my colleagues or my students.

In fact, Robert Boice's research on faculty productivity yielded interesting findings when he compared faculty who wrote without logging their time with faculty who wrote *and* logged their time. "By writing daily and keeping records the second group was able to outperform the first group by a factor of *four*," writes Tara Gray (2005, pp. 19–20), summarizing Boice's research. Even more interesting are Boice's findings regarding faculty who, besides logging their writing times regularly, also shared their logs with the researchers conducting the study. When compared, faculty who shared their writing logs were *9 times* more productive than the faculty who had only logged their times, without sharing the log with someone else (Boice, 1989; Gray, 2005)!

Where or in what format you record your writing time in each writing session makes little difference. Some of my students—as technologically savvy as they are—still prefer to log their times in small spiral-bound notebooks, which they always carry with them. Others (including me), like to use an electronic spreadsheet for tracking their time. I use MS Excel, as it allows me to run simple calculations if I want to. How many minutes did I write this week? How many hours did I write this month? How many minutes writing did I average per day, in the past month? You can answer simple questions such as these if you track using Excel or a similar spreadsheet. But you can also use word-processing software and log your writing time using a table. Bottom line: Customize the log for your way of thinking, preferences, and needs.

However, a few items you *do* want to keep track of are things such as the date, the time you began writing, and the time you stopped (I also like to have a column with the total minutes I spent writing in that session). Some people like to keep track of how many pages were written in each session; others like to record the number of words written (I don't particularly care for counting words because, during editing stages, I'm cutting down the text and it feels as though I'm writing less and less when, in fact, I'm polishing more and more!). It is important to note which writing project you worked on during the session you're recording: Write down something simple, such as "dissertation proposal" or "abstract for such-and-such conference." I like to have a column describing the project I intend to work on, as well as a column describing in brief detail what I actually accomplished during that particular writing session—for example, "Writing project: Manuscript with Carol; Accomplished: edited the methods section." At times, I also like to have a column to note where I should begin in the next writing session—for example, "Next time: Finish editing methods section." Finally, one of my students suggested the following idea, and I have used it ever since: Have a column where you can briefly note how you felt during that writing session. This helps you observe yourself as a writer and how you have felt while dealing with a specific writing project. Figure 2.1 gives you an example extracted from my writing log. I also placed a skeleton log on the book's website (www.sagepub.com/goodson).

Figure 2.1 Writing Log Example

MONTH	DAY	DAY/WEEK	YEAR	GOAL/WORK ON...	START TIME	STOP TIME	TOTAL MINUTES	ACCOMPLISHED
April	1	Friday	2011	C. Grant	7:10am	8:00am	50	Edited Module 2 (L.Os 1 - 3)
April	1	Friday	2011	Nomination Letter for M.	8:30am	8:45am	15	Edited and submitted
April	1	Friday	2011	Book	4:20pm	4:40pm	20	Working with chapters' sequence
April	2	Saturday	2011	C. Grant	9:50am	10:25am	35	Edited Module 3.1
April	2	Saturday	2011	C. Grant	10:45am	11:25am	40	Edited Module 3.2
April	2	Saturday	2011	C. Grant	3:00pm	4:05pm	65	COMPLETED C. MODULES!!!!!
April	2	Saturday	2011	Book	5:20pm	6:05pm	45	Working on re-structuring the contents
April	3	Sunday	2011	TP for class	9:20am	10:10am	50	Wrote 7 TPs
April	3	Sunday	2011	TP for class	12:10am	12:45pm	35	Wrote 5 TPs
April	3	Sunday	2011	Reviewing K's manuscript	4:30pm	5:15pm	45	Edited till first segment in Findings
April	4	Monday	2011	Book	6:40am	8:00am	80	Worked on revising the TOC
April	4	Monday	2011	Reviewing K's manuscript	8:30am	10:40am	130	Reviewed most of the paper/met w/K.
April	4	Monday	2011	Drafting P. G. #2	5:30pm	6:50pm	80	Began drafting second p. grant
April	5	Tuesday	2011	Book	6:50am	7:55am	65	Editing and re-formatting
April	5	Tuesday	2011	G. A. G. Reviews	5:30pm	7:00pm	90	Reviewing 3 grant proposals
April	6	Wednesday	2011	Book	6:50am	8:55am	65	Editing Chapter 2
April	7	Thursday	2011	Book	10:00am	11:05am	65	Editing Chapter 4
April	7	Thursday	2011	Reviewing R's chapter/dissert	11:15am	12:00pm	45	Reviewing

EXERCISE 6—READ ABOUT WRITING

TIME NEEDED: 10 minutes x session

MATERIALS NEEDED: Timer; a book about writing

Reading and writing go hand in hand. Reading other authors' good writing is an important ingredient in the recipe for writing well. Yet, invariably, when I raise this issue with my students, they retort: "And what, exactly, constitutes 'good' writing?" This is always a difficult question to address, apart from personal preferences for certain writing styles. My answer, however, has consistently pointed to three elements. First, good writing is the kind of writing we *want* to read, the kind that grabs us, speaks to us, and has us saying, deep in our hearts, "Oh, I wish I had written *that!*" (Rosenblatt, 2011). Second, good writing is well crafted, or writing in which the author was thoughtful and thorough: Words were carefully chosen, images were brilliantly drawn, connections were made in surprising and unexpected ways—all of it resulting in a new and refreshing approach to a topic.

Some would claim such artistry is more often found in fiction writing, or literature, rarely in academic writing. Many people claim academic writing has little room for creativity and is very formulaic or rigid regarding word choice and text structure. Yes, it is true. Academic writing follows rigorous standards because it cannot afford to be ambiguous or vague or imprecise. Poetry, on the other hand, does nothing *but* be ambiguous, intentionally. But being rigorous does not preclude writing with care, paying attention, and, when possible, using some surprising or unexpected images, arrangements of ideas, or special words (or even creating new words once in a while!).

Finally, good writing is the kind that inspires us to carry on our own writing! Here, I'm thinking specifically of books *about writing* that discuss the craft, its struggles and joys: texts that teach us a trick or two about writing better or writing more. For this week's exercise, I'll focus on this latter type of good writing.

This week's exercise involves three steps:

1. Identify a book about writing, which you might want to read.

2. Read that book for 10 minutes, at the beginning of your writing sessions. Use your timer, and do not exceed the 10-minute limit. Be careful not to turn your writing session into a reading session.

3. If in the book you find an idea or suggestion you think will be useful (or at least worth trying), note the idea in writing. (You may want to start a writing

journal, someplace you can make notes to yourself about your reading, writing, and exercises.) Incorporate that particular suggestion in today's writing session, if possible.

Good books *about* writing abound in the market today! You'll find several types of books to choose from: famous writers' memoirs or biographies, detailing their writing lives and the strategies they use to write; books that present entire writing workshops and models for writing; books providing tips on grammar, punctuation, spelling, and editing; books containing warm-up exercises; books on how to write particular products, such as book proposals, textbooks, journal articles, or grant proposals for funding; and books on how to write for therapeutic purposes (to deal with personal trauma, for instance) or for personal growth.

Pick a book. Any book. At the end of *this* book I provide a list of those I have read and highly recommend. Choose one. If you can ask for someone's recommendation, even better. If you choose a book and you don't like it in the first few pages, stop. Get another one. Don't waste precious time reading material that doesn't help, motivate, or touch you. Life is way too short to read all the good writing available let alone to waste time reading what doesn't help.

This is one exercise you might incorporate routinely into your writing sessions (at least once a day). Continue reading until you finish one book. Then, either take a break from reading or start another one. The advice contained in the books, coupled with the sheer motivation to keep on writing, will be worth the 10-minute investment you'll make. I guarantee.

On a final note: C. S. Lewis, author of *The Chronicles of Narnia*, once said we read to learn we are not alone (http://www.goodreads.com/author/quotes/1069006.C_S_Lewis). Because writing can be a very lonely task, reading about writing will remind us we are not alone. As you read other authors' reflections on the "writing life" (Dillard, 1989), you will find yourself comforted and supported by people who have struggled with the same issues you are struggling with now. Who knows, maybe someday you'll be writing your own book, telling the world your own story of struggling with writing—and overcoming!

EXERCISE 7—DOCUMENT YOUR WRITING PROJECTS

TIME NEEDED: 10 minutes x session (05 at the beginning, 05 at the end)

MATERIALS NEEDED: Timer

Keeping a log of my writing sessions helps provide a concrete, objective sense of the time I spend writing, which projects I tackle each time, and what I accomplish in each session. I know no other positive reinforcement that works so well in keeping me motivated and attuned to how much I have actually written!

Nevertheless, I also have learned it is useful to have a mechanism for capturing the decisions I make throughout a project, a place to write notes to myself regarding items I need to check, and a system for recording the development of a particular writing piece over time. I have, therefore, learned to keep writing diaries as a mechanism and a place for document-ing my progress.

All my writing projects have their own diary or journal: a Word file in which I make entries every time I work on them. When I begin a writing session using my computer, the very *first* file I open is my writing log; the *second* file, the journal; and the *third* file, the actual writing project. In my diary I write as little or as much as I need to, but I try to capture the gist of the moment. I first date the entry, then write the goals for that particular writing session. When I end my writing session, before I record the end time in my writing log, I return to the diary to note what I accomplished and to leave a note to myself, such as "*Tomorrow:* begin at point X and add data Y to the first paragraph." This simple note allows me to pick up where I left off, without any need to waste time recalling, *Where did I stop last time?* or *What was I supposed to do next?*

I borrowed this idea of writing diaries from my habit of maintaining a data-analysis journal for every research study I conduct, regardless if the analyses are quantitative or qualitative. I cannot tell you how many times these diaries have saved my life—especially in instances when I've been away from a particular project for a while. What I mean by "saved my life" is, these journals either contain evidence to support a decision I made in the past or describe the reasons underlying specific analytic choices I once made. Trying to recall why I created a new variable at a certain point in the study, how I constructed that variable, or which statistical tests contained the new variable—all these steps might be fresh in my mind as I'm conduct-ing the analysis. But 3 weeks later the entire process is a blur, and I cannot remember the details of my reasoning.

Because I strongly encourage you to document the progression of your writing projects, the exercise this week entails setting up and getting used to writing about your project in a diary or journal. You will need to do the following:

1. Open a new Word file and label it "journal" or "diary." If you are not using a computer, designate a new notebook especially for the purpose of journaling, and take notes by hand.

2. Document today's date on the first page (day, month, and year).

3. Briefly jot down what you wish to accomplish during today's writing session.

4. If you are struggling with the project or have questions you must answer before moving ahead, make note of these struggles and questions. Talk to yourself, here, about the project: your goals, concerns, accomplishments. Use this moment to dump or capture random thoughts about the project, if you wish. You can always copy and paste the useful ideas into your project's file later.

5. When you have situated yourself and know exactly what to do, move on to your regular writing session.

6. When your session ends, before you log the end time in your writing log, return to your diary.

7. Make note of what you were able to accomplish during your regular writing session.

8. Before closing the file, write down what you will need to do *tomorrow*. Be as specific as you can. "Tomorrow" may actually mean several days from now, and you need all the help you can get remembering precisely where you left off.

9. Be sure to capture important decisions you made today regarding your project and/or decisions you will need to make soon. Remember: Documenting your reasoning behind specific choices may prove useful, in the future, if you have to explain or justify them.

Example

Below, you'll find an excerpt from the journal I maintained while writing this book. Notice how simple it is. Despite its simplicity, however, the journal helped me *never* experience writer's block while crafting the book, because I always knew where to begin, each and every time!

Even when I navigate among several different writing tasks simultaneously, I know precisely where I stopped in every project and where to return—no difficulties remembering or keeping track of what to do where. I need not waste any time warming up or trying to get back into a given piece: The notes I leave are enough to guide me precisely where I need to go, to restart the writing. It's like a "You Are Here" map at the shopping mall, red dot and all!

April 10, 2011

Today: continue editing chapter 4—doing the key sentence file. D finished editing Chapter 3. So as soon as I finish 4, I'll send it off to him. Once I've done up till chapter 5, need to go back and re-check the intro, and chapters 1–3.

Okay . . . worked on the key sentence file (and editing) of Chapter 4, but still have not finished it. Stopped at Exercise 20 (the last one, I believe).

Tomorrow: Finish key sentence file for Chapter 4—read key sentence file, then make edits. Read Chapter 4 out loud again. Submit to D for review.

April 12, 2011

Today: finish key sentence file for chapter 4. Read Chapter 4 out loud.

Okay: finished key sentences file and incorporated edits into Chapter 4.

Tomorrow: read out loud once more. Submit to D. for review.

April 13, 2011

Today: read chapter 4 out loud once more. Sent to D. for review.

Okay. . . . Read up to the end of Exercise 18.

Tomorrow: Need to read Exercises 19 and 20, and add Research Shows box to this chapter.

EXERCISE 8—WRITE TO LEARN (ANYTHING, INCLUDING HOW TO WRITE)

TIME NEEDED: 10–15 minutes x session

MATERIALS NEEDED: Timer

Although writing is—unequivocally—THE most important tool for success in academic settings, we often relegate it exclusively to the professional dimension of our lives. Its value in facilitating other dimensions of everyday living is quite often ignored. This exercise, therefore, will help you think about writing as a tool for living a successful life, both inside and outside academia. Writing, for instance, can become your most important tool for learning.[1] Here's how.

William Zinsser—who authored many acclaimed texts, including *On Writing Well* (2006)[2]—wrote a gem of a book called *Writing to Learn* (1988). In this text, Zinsser explores using writing for learning just about *anything*. He grounds the narrative in his personal experience trying to learn certain topics in school, his growth as a writer, and his later adventures as a writing professor at Yale. He writes, introducing his text to the reader:

> The writing of [this] book proved one of its central points: that we write to find out what we know and what we want to say. I thought of how often as a writer I had made clear to myself some subject I had previously known nothing about by just putting one sentence after another—by reasoning my way in sequential steps to its meaning. I thought of how often the act of writing even the simplest document—a letter, for instance—had clarified my half-formed ideas. **Writing and thinking and learning were the same process.** (pp. viii–ix; emphasis added)

I strongly encourage you to read Zinsser's book, of course, but for now, think about it . . . when was the last time you tried to understand a difficult topic or think your way through a complex personal problem by writing about it, by placing one sentence after another? Probably not recently. And why not? Why don't we resort to "thinking on paper" (as I like to refer to it) more often, more naturally, more automatically?

My best answer to this question is, we just haven't been socialized into the practice. We haven't been taught how to do it, or how to value it. Western thinking prizes the image of knowledge building we associate with Greek culture: intellectuals in public spaces, engaging in lively *debates* or *conversations,* oozing wisdom at every syllable; teaching while walking along the way (*peripatetically,* as Aristotle and his followers would call it); debating, debating . . . Thus, for us who inhabit Western cultures, our image of knowledge development is rarely associated with *writing;* it's more often associated with *talking* or *discussing.* When we think of ancient scholars bent over their parchments, writing away, we tend to think of *copying*—of the scribes in biblical times who wrote letters dictated by others, who laboriously copied ancient text, letter by letter, with modern-day copying-machine precision. We rarely associate *those* images of writing with knowledge development, knowledge building. And because this is our intellectual inheritance, we are socialized into thinking, first, then copying and pasting our thoughts into a written medium, much like taking dictation from ourselves.

We rarely view writing as the tool that builds the edifice of our knowledge, that helps construct the scaffold in which we stand to survey a new landscape. We have not learned how to build knowledge using writing, nor have we learned how to prepare our writing tool for such a task. Many of us (dare I say, almost all of us?) have not learned how to write, especially how to *write to think* and how to *write to learn.*

This week's exercise, therefore, will help you begin taking the first steps in a new direction: using writing to think and to learn—anything. I can't help but invoke Zinsser (1988), once more, to help make the point clear:

> Contrary to general belief, writing isn't something that only "writers" do; writing is a basic skill for getting through life. (p. 11)

> Writing organizes and clarifies our thoughts. Writing is how we think our way into a subject and make it our own. Writing enables us to find out what we know—and what we don't know—about whatever we're trying to learn. (p. 16)

For this exercise, you should choose a topic with which you are not familiar: something you'd *like* to learn more about, a topic you *need* to learn more about, or an issue you feel the desire to explore (either to help you make a decision or to help someone else navigate through a particular struggle)—something new to you. This something could be a dimension of the research project you're currently working on or one aspect of that literature review you've been dreading because you just don't know what to look for.

The exercise consists of writing about this unknown, yet-to-be-understood subject every day for 10 to 15 minutes as part of your writing sessions. What will you write about? Begin with *"I don't have a clue what I'm going to say about _____ (subject) yet. It's completely new to me. I do know I need to understand this better, because . . ."* Begin by writing what the topic seems to be about (you may not even know the precise terminology for writing about it, yet, and that's perfectly fine!). Write how you feel about it, what you think you want to know, what you *do in fact know,* and, especially, what you don't know and need to learn. This represents an exercise in honesty, above all else: being honest with yourself and admitting you don't know something you should have known well by now. It doesn't matter if you *should* have known it; the reality is, you don't know it. So you're going to learn about it.

As you determine which elements you need to learn more about, list those in writing. After your writing session ends, make it a point to begin to learn, step-by-step, about each element you listed in your writing. Read. Research. But don't just read and research: Write about what you're reading (*as you are reading,* preferably); write about what you're researching. Note your discoveries; explain new concepts to yourself—always in writing—until you get it. You will know you "got it" when you can write easily and freely about that one concept you were trying to understand.

Example

Here's an example of what I wrote when trying to learn all I could learn about self-esteem and how it's been assessed among adolescents, within the public health research literature. I realized my understanding of the self-esteem construct was quite fuzzy when I decided to review systematically the studies exploring the relationships among self-esteem, sexual intentions, attitudes, and sexual behaviors among adolescents. Had someone asked me to define self-esteem, I probably couldn't have gone beyond the idea of "how much one likes one's self." I had to be honest and admit: although I had great plans for reviewing the literature, I lacked basic knowledge regarding the self-esteem construct. I decided to slow down and learn all I could about it, beginning with its definition—or, as I would later learn, with its multiple, slightly different definitions. (Note: Learning there were multiple definitions, with nuanced variations, had important implications for my review.) Here's an excerpt from my writing-to-learn process, at the time.

I need to provide the definitions of self esteem (SE) here.

Also need to discuss whether SE is a stable or variable trait. What is it? Stable or variable? I don't quite know. Can it change? Researchers debate whether it is possible to change SE or not; Harter (in Baumeister's edited book), for instance, while acknowledging that some authors do not believe self-esteem can change—believes, herself, that SE is amenable to change, especially among children and adolescents at specific times in their lives when the self is re-evaluated (coinciding, often times with changes in school grade levels); however, she demonstrates some skepticism concerning the possibility of change, when self-esteem scores are particularly low, especially if the individuals lack social and emotional support to sustain any kind of change. Interesting . . .

You will notice how unpolished the paragraph above sounds—and because I didn't write it for anyone else to read, it is just that: unpolished. But it captured my thinking as I was learning about self-esteem, as I raised specific questions regarding what I *didn't know* and, therefore, needed to learn. By the way, the question of whether SE is stable or variable is not yet resolved among scholars; the debate continues, as most good debates in the social sciences do.

You get the idea. You write your thoughts, and as you learn something, you express those thoughts in simple, declarative sentences, bit by bit, arranging your knowledge in a logical format, focusing on communicating clearly. Practice this writing every day for a few days, and I guarantee your knowledge on a given subject will increase or deepen. No doubt about it!

Notes

1. Writing is equally helpful for healing from psychological traumas. A whole body of literature describes the benefits of writing about traumatic events and the healing that often results from such writing. If you would like to begin exploring that literature, read Janet Conner's (2008) *Writing Down Your Soul.* She compiles and comments on much of the available research on writing as a tool for healing.

2. This book, alone, has sold more than 1 million copies since its first edition 30 years ago, *without* advertising (McCutcheon, 2006, p. 25)!

Electronic Sources

Goodreads, C. S. Lewis Quotes: http://www.goodreads.com/author/quotes/1069006.C_S_Lewis

References

Albarracin, D., Johnson, B. T., & Zanna, M. P. (Eds.). (2005). *The handbook of attitudes.* Mahwah, NJ: Lawrence Erlbaum.

Boice, R. (1983). Contingency management in writing and the appearance of creative ideas. *Behaviour Research and Therapy, 21, 537–543.*

Boice, R. (1989). Procrastination, busyness and bingeing. *Behaviour Research and Therapy, 27*(6), 605–611.

Boice, R. (1997a). Strategies for enhancing scholarly productivity. In J. M. Moxley & T. Taylor (Eds.), *Writing and publishing for academic authors* (2nd ed., pp. 19–34). Lanham, MD: Rowman & Littlefield.

Boice, R. (1997b). Which is more productive, writing in binge patterns of creative illness or in moderation? *Written Communication, 14*(4), 435–459.

Carr, N. (2011). *The shallows: What the Internet is doing to our brains.* New York: W. W. Norton.

Cleary, T. J., & Zimmerman, B. J. (2001). Self-regulation differences during athletic practice by experts, non-experts, and novices. *Journal of Applied Sport Psychology, 13*(2), 185–206.

Colvin, G. (2010). *Talent is overrated: What really separates world-class performers from everybody else.* New York: Portfolio (Penguin Group).

Conner, J. (2008). *Writing down your soul: How to activate and listen to the extraordinary voice within.* San Francisco: Conari Press.

Coyle, D. (2009). *The talent code: Greatness isn't born. It's grown. Here's how.* New York: Bantam Dell.

Dillard, A. (1989). *The writing life.* New York: HarperPerennial.

Elbow, P. (1998). *Writing with power: Techniques for mastering the writing process* (2nd ed.). New York: Oxford University Press.

Ericsson, K. A. (2007). Deliberate practice and the modifiability of body and mind: Toward a science of the structure and acquisition of expert and elite performance. *International Journal of Sport Psychology, 38,* 4–34.

Ericsson, K. A. (2008). Deliberate practice and acquisition of expert performance: A general overview. *Academic Emergency Medicine, 15,* 988–994.

Ericsson, K. A., Nandagopal, K., & Roring, R. W. (2009). Toward a science of exceptional achievement: Attaining superior performance through deliberate practice. *Longevity, Regeneration, and Optimal Health: Ann. N.Y. Acad. Sci., 1172,* 199–217.

Gray, T. (2005). *Publish & flourish.* Springfield, IL: Teaching Academy, New Mexico State University.

Johnson, W. B., & Mullen, C. A. (2007). *Write to the top! How to become a prolific academic.* New York: Palgrave McMillan.

Kitsantas, A., & Zimmerman, B. J. (2006). Enhancing self-regulation of practice: The influence of graphing and self-evaluative standards. *Metacognition and Learning, 1*(3), 201–212.

Mayrath, M. (2008). Attributions of productive authors in educational psychology journals. *Educational Psychology Review, 20,* 41–56.

McCutcheon, M. (2006). *Damn! Why didn't I write that?* (2nd ed.). Clovis, CA: Quill Driver Books.

Medina, J. (2008). *Brain rules: 12 principles for surviving and thriving at work, home, and school.* Seattle, WA: Pear Press.

Mikhailova, E. A., & Nilson, L. B. (2007). Developing prolific scholars: The "fast article writing" methodology. *Journal of Faculty Development, 21*(2), 93–100.

Rosenblatt, R. (2011). *Unless it moves the human heart: The craft and art of writing.* New York: HarperCollins.

Zimmerman, B. J., & Kitsantas, A. (1999). Acquiring writing revision skill: Shifting from process to outcome self-regulatory goals. *Journal of Educational Psychology, 91*(2), 241–250.

Zinsser, W. (1988). *Writing to learn: How to write—and think—clearly about any subject at all.* New York: Harper & Row.

Zinsser, W. (2006). *On writing well: The classic guide to writing nonfiction* (30th anniversary ed.). New York: "HarperCollins.

Chapter Three

Practice Building Academic Vocabulary

Summary

Think About It . . .

EXERCISE 9—Increase Your Vocabulary One Word at a Time

EXERCISE 10—Use New Academic Words

EXERCISE 11—Build Your Own Professional Dictionary/Glossary

Writing is easy.

All you have to do is cross out the wrong words.

Mark Twain (1835–1910)

Think About It . . .

Vocabulary . . . the library of words we use to think, talk, and write; defined in a dictionary as

> words used by a particular language, individual, book, branch of science, etc., or by a particular author; list of these [words] arranged alphabetically with definitions or translations. (*Oxford Desk Dictionary and Thesaurus*, 1997, p. 903)

And what, exactly, is a word? The same reliable dictionary defines *words* as sounds combined or organized into meaningful units of speech or writing. Words, therefore, connect sounds (or letters) to meanings in specific ways.

But language philosophers like to point out that words are more than mere labels or tags we slap on objects and phenomena around us. Words *define* reality; while they label the physical entities in our world, words also *create* meanings, *create* phenomena for which no physical corresponding object exists. Words, thus, both *name* and *create* the world around and within us.

Here's an example of a word that creates a reality existing nowhere else but in the word itself: a *promise*. Think about it: Promises occur only in the world of language. You cannot point to anything in your physical environment and say, "Here: this is a promise." You can show me the *fulfillment* of the promise but never the promise itself. If I promise to take you out to dinner tonight, you can—at dinner—say something like, "Here we are. Just as you promised." But what we're experiencing at dinner is the fulfillment or object of the promise, not the *promise itself*. The promise itself came to life only when I talked about it, in the words I used to make it: "I promise we will go out to dinner tonight." Outside these words, the promise didn't exist. If I had never said (or written) them, I wouldn't have made a promise.

Academic words such as *analysis, theory,* and *hypothesis* also are examples of realities subsisting merely in the language world. Theories are a good example: A theory—defined as a story about the cause-and-effect relationships among factors, elements, or events—exists only as language (Goodson, 2010). One cannot point to a slide under a microscope and exclaim, "Here's the theory of evolution." We can point only to evidence to support a theory, not to the theory itself. We can *see* the theory only when we tell the story. The only way to visualize the theory is to listen to, or read, the words that shape it.

Words, therefore, are much more powerful than we care to admit. As Brazilian philosopher Rubem Alves (1979) points out:

> Language functions as a mediation tool between humans and their world. As humans, we don't contemplate reality face-to-face. Since birth, things in our world don't come to us in their naked form, but always dressed up in the names our community has given them. This community has already defined how and what the world is like and, therefore, already knows it (the world). This knowledge of the world is crystallized in our language. Language, therefore, is not a copy of objects and facts. Language is always *interpretation*. (p. 54)

Some scholars believe language defines reality in such a way that it even shapes what our brains are able to *see*. Yes, I'm talking about the physical act of seeing, the light hitting our retinas and forming a specific object in our line of vision. If we don't have a word for that object, say these scholars, our brains don't recognize it, don't *see* it. For example: Let's say you and I have developed a friendship over e-mail, but we've never met face-to-face. We decide it's time to get together and meet each other, so we schedule time at a coffeehouse tomorrow, 10 in the morning. I try to describe to you how I look so you'll be able to recognize me. If I use words such as *tall, blonde hair, tan, wearing a white shirt* to describe myself, you will not see me when I walk through the door of the coffeehouse. I am petite, brunette, wearing a blue blouse. Your eyes will be guided to see only tall, blonde women wearing a white shirt. It will take you a few seconds to register if I stop, turn to you, and say, "Hi! Waiting for Pat Goodson?" Your vision, your ability to see, will be entirely shaped by the description I have given you. The words preclude your eyes from seeing anything else.

Such is the power of words: They shape our reality, *determine* what we see and what we don't see, mold our points of view, guide our eyes. A rather strong force, these bits of language!

But words not only shape our ability to see/not see reality, they also carry cultural meanings and interpretations. One quick example: the Portuguese word *saudade*. The term describes the feelings associated with missing someone who's absent, or longing for a place we haven't visited in quite some time; the feelings of missing some*one* but also missing some*thing* from the past, something especially dear to us, such as our home country. The word doesn't translate well into English. In English we need multiple phrases to *explain* the term, whereas Portuguese speakers know exactly what kind of a feeling is being referred to when one utters the term *saudade*. There's no need to explain. The word exists only in the Portuguese language (so I have been told), and only one African language has an equivalent: *banzo* (the term African slaves used for describing their longing for their native land, associated with sadness, emptiness, and powerlessness). Words such as *saudade* and *banzo* embody their cultural heritage, their history, their geography. They carry within them much more than just an idea or concept. They incorporate a tradition, a way of feeling, a history and geography of sorts. Their meanings, therefore, are inevitably lost in translation.

Once we agree that words convey cultural meanings, it is easier to acknowledge that learning a new language is also learning a new culture. Along with the words (and the grammar by which they are arranged into phrases or sentences), we learn about a particular cultural group's interpretation of its reality—quite often very different from our own language and interpretations.

But what does this view of language have to do with building academic vocabulary?

Here's how the two elements connect: Learning a specific vocabulary for a given academic field involves a bifurcated experience. It requires learning the *technical terminology* the field employs and learning about the *world as seen or interpreted by that particular field*. This makes learning academic vocabulary a complex task—it involves acquiring both a construct and its embedded cultural values.

Have you noticed how much technical vocabulary you need to master when you're trying to learn something new? I'm always amazed! Take statistics, for instance. Most of my graduate students have a love/hate relationship with statistics. Their ambivalent feelings begin when confronted with the new language they have to master. Terms such as *mean, average,* and *median* have more or less made it into colloquial language, but when it comes to terms such as *confidence intervals, stochastic models, simple classical probability, homoscedasticity, Poisson distribution, latent structure,* and *general linear model*, a student has no doubt stepped into a new world, a new culture, not merely a new language. A colleague of mine at Texas A&M University, Dr. Bruce Thompson (2006)—a Distinguished Professor in our College of Education and Human Development—has mercifully come to the rescue of graduate students and explained the issues surrounding statistical terminology:

> The language of statistics is intentionally designed to confuse the graduate students (and everyone else). This mischievousness takes various forms. . . . First, some terms have different meanings in different contexts. . . . Second, we use multiple synonymous names for the same terms. . . . Of course, at the annual summer statistical convention (called a *conven*), which statistics professors

regularly attend to make our language even more confusing, an important agreement was reached long, long ago. It is not reasonable to confuse the graduate students on unimportant terms. Thus, we have more synonymous terms for the most important concepts, and consequently the importance of a concept can be intuited by counting the number of recognized synonymous terms for the concept. (pp. 4–5)

As if learning a single term for a single concept weren't complex enough!!! I hear you, graduate students! Been there myself.

And so it happens when we're beginners in any field: We must master new terminology, regardless of how obscure or confusing it may sound. Mastering new terminologies as well as their built-in cultures, however, happens slowly and through exposure to what we *read* or *hear:* classic texts, research reports, conference proceedings, classroom and meeting presentations. And it is not until we *use* the new terminology ourselves that we know we have captured the new concepts with all their complexity and nuances. It is when we use the new terminology in our writing, therefore, that we determine how much we truly grasp our own discipline.

As we gradually master the new vocabulary in our respective fields, we find it becomes easier to write about certain topics. But if we don't *continually* challenge ourselves to learn new words, to try new ways to say the same old things, our writing eventually becomes stale and boring. That's why stretching ourselves—vocabularywise—should be an academic writer's lifelong pursuit. And it need not be a stressful one; it can be done in microdoses, almost imperceptibly. The exercises in this section are designed to do just that: stretch your vocabulary base without much stress, have you learning new words without much suffering. In time, you can become a "walking thesaurus" without much effort (we'll talk about using a thesaurus to write later on).

Tip for ESL Writers

Most of my foreign students admit they are not familiar with a thesaurus. So, I'd like to use this space to introduce thesauri (plural of thesaurus) to ESL writers and point out how they can effectively improve one's writing!

The word *thesaurus* comes from the Greek language and means "treasure store." A most appropriate label for this treasure of a resource!

A thesaurus is different from a dictionary. In a dictionary, we find the definitions of specific words and their pronunciations. A thesaurus, on the other hand, lists words that are similar in meaning (but not necessarily *identical* in meaning). Most thesauri list both synonyms *and* antonyms. Thesauri, therefore, are extremely helpful to find an alternate term for your text when you want to avoid repeating the same word. For instance, instead of writing *research,* you can also use *inquiry, search, quest, pursuit, examination, review, scrutiny, investigation, exploration, analysis.* Notice that the terms *research* and *analysis,* for example, differ substantially in their definitions, but for our academic writing we can frequently use these words interchangeably.

You can purchase a bound thesaurus or you can use the ones available on the Internet. My favorite one is *Roget's Thesaurus of English Words and Phrases,* available at http://poets.notredame.ac.jp/Roget/.

NOTE: Specialized thesauri are available in many disciplines. For example, *Evaluation Thesaurus, Thesaurus of Psychological Index Terms* (APA), *Art and Architecture Thesaurus.* Check out if your discipline has one! It will become your new best friend, I'm sure!

EXERCISE 9—INCREASE YOUR VOCABULARY ONE WORD AT A TIME

TIME NEEDED: 15 minutes x session

MATERIALS NEEDED: Timer; vocabulary website or dictionary

This week's exercise will focus on helping you incorporate new words into your writing. For now, these new words will not necessarily be technical terms (we'll leave technical vocabulary for our next exercise). Here, we will practice with nontechnical English words or phrases you might not normally use.

To begin, you need to enroll in a website that sends one new word every day to your e-mail. Various sites offer this for free. I have signed up for two such services (one is free; the other is not).

The free service is called Vocab Vitamins (http://www.vocabvitamins .com). The site offers several options: one free word-a-day newsletter or a paid newsletter containing pronunciation and practice tools.

The paid service is called Visual Thesaurus (http://www.visualthesaurus .com). I will mention this site, again, in Exercise 24 when I talk about using a thesaurus to write. The site offers many services and tips that are useful for writers of all genres. If you choose to subscribe (for a modest annual fee), you will receive one word a day in your e-mail, along with access to much useful information for authors.

When you receive your first word, you are ready to begin the exercise. Please note: If you do not have access to the Internet, you can use a bound dictionary and randomly pick a word, every day, to practice this exercise.

1. Read about your new word (if possible, listen to how it is pronounced), learn about its origins, and check how it has been used in published texts by taking a close look at the examples provided (if they are provided).

2. For the next few minutes, practice *using* that word in sentences you might write in your journal articles, research reports, or grant proposals. Try to write three or four different sentences using that particular word. Develop sentences similar to those you might use in your academic writing.

Alternative

After you receive (or randomly pick from the dictionary) your word of the day:

1. Read and learn about it as much as you can (see #1 above).

2. Write it down somewhere, then begin your daily writing session. Challenge yourself to use the new word at least once in your writing that day. Your usage may not be perfect today; don't worry, you can always edit it out later. For now, however, try to apply it somewhere in an intelligible manner.

Example

As I write this chapter, my word of the day arrived in my e-mail inbox. Today's word is *consonance,* defined as harmony, agreement, accord, or congruity (http://www.vocabvitamins.com). When I try to use the term in four different sentences, here's what I come up with (notice, I'm trying to use the term in sentences I would normally write in my academic journal articles or reports):

1. Findings from this study are in *consonance* with most available literature on the topic.

2. In *consonance* with our findings, Smith's study proposes equally challenging results.

3. Our main argument—in *consonance* with most current thinking on the topic—emphasizes the need for further in-depth study.

4. While our points of view may be contested by many scholars, they are in *consonance* with the latest research findings in this area.

> ### *Research Shows . . .*
>
> R. Boice (1997) conducted a study with 16 recently hired faculty members from departments in the humanities, social sciences, and hard sciences across various campuses. One group (of 8) wrote the way they always did, in binges (with "few breaks and with a hurried pace—a gait that they reported . . . as highly euphoric and essential to their best, most brilliant writing"; p. 444). The other group (of 8) wrote regularly (at least three times x week).
>
> Comparing the two groups, Boice documented the following: "Binge writers (a) accomplished far less writing overall, (b) got fewer editorial acceptances, (c) scored higher on the Beck Depression Inventory, and (d) listed fewer creative ideas for writing" (p. 435).

It took about 5 minutes to develop these four sentences. I confess, however, it wasn't very easy. *Consonance* is not a word I would normally use in my academic writing. I would have preferred using *agreement, in line with,* or variations of these terms. Nevertheless, I now know that *consonance* is a nice alternative, especially if I'm trying to avoid repeating the word *agreement.*

Caution! It's fun to master new vocabulary and employ exactly the right word for the right phenomenon (just like having the right tool for the right job). It is so much fun, in fact, that we can be tempted to show off in our writing how many polysyllable words we know. I have learned, however, that I should never assume my readers will know the meaning of words that are used more infrequently in writing. Therefore, to be safe and ensure your communication is crystal clear, always (always!) take the time to define the new words you want to use if you suspect some readers may be unfamiliar with them. Usually a short parenthetical explanation will do. In the example above, just to be sure readers will understand the meaning of the word *consonance,* I might use it in a sentence where I also use the phrase *in agreement with.* This way, readers can conclude, on their own, that *consonance* and *in agreement with* have similar meanings, without my having to define it.

And remember the following:

1. One way to check whether your new words communicate or make readers stumble through your reading is to **get feedback** on what you write (more on getting feedback later, in Chapter 5).

2. If you turn this exercise into a habit, you may **increase your vocabulary by at least 300 words a year.** In 10 years, you will have added a minimum of 3,000 new terms to your vocabulary—not a trivial feat, even if some scholars estimate the English language has between 250,000 and 1,000,000 nontechnical words (depending on how they're counted—see http://www.oxforddictionaries .com/page/93 and Payack, 2008).

EXERCISE 10—USE NEW ACADEMIC WORDS

TIME NEEDED: 15 minutes for the first session; 10 minutes x session thereafter

MATERIALS NEEDED: Timer; well-written, published journal article(s) in your field

When you first do this exercise, develop a list of words commonly used in your field. To create the list, choose one or two published journal articles. Take no more than 15 minutes to develop the list. Read the articles and jot down the nouns, adjectives, adverbs, and verbs used in these publications. I have provided an example of such a list below. Preferably, choose words you are not familiar with or words you normally do not use in your own writing.

Nouns, Adjectives, Adverbs	Verbs
1. Politically	1. Categorize
2. Attitude(s)	2. Explain
3. Factor	3. Correlate
4. Survey (use as a noun or a verb)	4. Predict
5. Pattern (use as a noun or a verb)	5. Discuss
6. Genetic	6. Provide
7. Conclusion	7. Facilitate
8. Antecedent	8. Revolve
9. Spectrum	
10. Connection	
11. Episode	
12. Significant	

For every practice session this week, do the following:

1. Choose three words from each column (three nouns, adjectives, or adverbs and three verbs).

2. During the time remaining to complete your 10 minutes, write generatively (really fast, without stopping). Use the six words you selected in your

writing. It doesn't matter what you're writing about: personal writing or your writing project(s).

3. Make sure you understand those words' precise meanings and how to use them (check the article from which you drew the words or consult a dictionary).

Example

I chose the report of a study done by Brett Smith and Andrew C. Sparkes (2005), titled "Men, Sport, Spinal Cord Injury, and Narratives of Hope."

While reading the article, instead of developing my list with two columns, I decided to broaden things a bit, so I developed four columns: one for verbs, one for adjectives/adverbs, one for transitions, and one for phrases I found particularly interesting but do not often use in my own writing.

Verbs	Adjectives/ Adverbs	Transitions	Phrases
Draw (drawing on data)	Disruptive	Despite	Sustained efforts
Instigate	Ubiquitous	In contrast	A number of
Argue	Thematic	At the start of	scholars have
Suggest	Confidential	Further	pointed out
Grapple	Concrete	During	Against this
Operate	Unfamiliar	With regard to	backdrop
Frame	Presumably	Finally	Social vacuum
Enact	Aspired to	Accordingly	Chart a course
Constrain		Similarly	
Enable			
Instill			

Then, I tried to generate sentences using one word from each of the four columns. Here are some sentences I generated while writing freely:

1. I **grapple** with **unfamiliar** terminology, **despite sustained efforts** to master new vocabulary.

2. Findings from this study seem to **argue** against other, **ubiquitous** evidence. **Further** comparisons between our data and existing evidence may **chart a course** toward resolving the apparent conflict.

3. We **frame** the arguments in the report in a **presumably concrete** manner. **At the start of** our reporting, we make clear the need for tangible, operational hypotheses; ones the reader can visualize and measure easily.

How you choose to format the list of new words is irrelevant, but aim to use between four and six new words every time you practice this exercise.

Will using a new set of words every day really help build vocabulary? Wouldn't it be best to practice using a single word, several times, in order to better remember it? These are some valid questions.

Keep in mind, though, the purpose of the exercise is to allow your mind/ brain to become familiar with new words while, at the same time, practicing using these words. The exercise also has the goal of helping your mind make associations among, and recall, the words you already know. It's almost like building your own mental thesaurus of similarly connected words and meanings (see Exercise 24 for more on thesauri). As you add a new word to your already existing mental list, your brain brings up the old list, reminding you of similar terms you have filed away in your memory. It's like the new-kid-on-the-block phenomenon: One of the old kids comes out to meet the new kid, then, suddenly, everyone comes out! This way, you build your vocabulary without the need to memorize anything. The new words settle into their new homes, into your working vocabulary, without much effort and, after a bit, become old friends!

EXERCISE 11—BUILD YOUR OWN PROFESSIONAL DICTIONARY/GLOSSARY

TIME NEEDED: 20 minutes x session

MATERIALS NEEDED: Timer; published materials in your field (journal articles or books)

When I began my PhD training in health education and came face-to-face with its new-to-me vocabulary, a helpful strategy I employed was developing my own glossary or dictionary of new terms. *Glossary* is defined as "a list of terms in a special subject, field, or area of usage, with accompanying definitions" (http://dictionary.reference.com/browse/glossary). I vividly remember beginning a course related to health promotion in communities and organizations, and struggling with the assigned readings. The reason I struggled? The terminology. Most of the material pertained to the fields of organizational culture and community building/community organizing. Nearly all readings were theoretical in nature, discussing—in very abstract language—many concepts, constructs, and the relationships among them. Once in a while, a few articles reported examples applying (or testing) these theories—and *those* examples helped me understand the theory much more clearly! But good examples were few and far between. I had to master the terminology by going outside the texts if I wanted to grasp the content.

Moreover, I soon learned that part of my struggle came from deceiving myself into thinking I *knew* what the words meant. It took me a while to realize that authors were using certain colloquial terms in technical ways. For instance, take the term *community building*. In everyday language a reader would most likely understand the phrase in terms of actual construction: building homes or other architectural infrastructure within a specific geographical area. Yet, in health education/health promotion, *community building* refers to "a process that people in a community engage in themselves" to bring about beneficial changes to their community. Community building is, therefore, a process and, some would even say, a *method* for enacting social change (Minkler, 1997; Minkler & Wallerstein, 1997).

To solve the problem with terminology, I developed my own dictionary of terms. Personal computers were not as popular at the time, so I just bought myself a notebook for recording addresses or phone numbers (the ones that come with alphabetized sections) and began writing down each term's definition, according to the definitions provided in the texts. As I did this, my understanding deepened and I also began to learn the nuances, those slight differences in meaning emerging from different authors' uses of the terms. Therefore, I also started to make note of who's defining what: this definition, for this term, comes from this particular author (Author X). When I came across a different definition, I would add it to my glossary, noting, "This second definition—which varies from the first one in this way—comes from Author Y."

Over time, my personal glossary made the readings in the class a lot easier. I strongly believe they also allowed for a depth of learning I had not experienced in my previous courses. Toward the end of that semester, I used the glossary less and less. I noticed the terms began repeating themselves, and I had developed full command of the diverse ways in which they were defined or used by different writers.

Because I believe my experience can be useful for your writing, too, I developed the following exercise. I highly recommend the exercise whenever you are learning a new topic or when you are attempting to build precision in your academic vocabulary.

NOTE: This exercise can be done together with the previous exercises. As you develop your personal glossary, you can use the glossary terms in Exercises 9 and 10, applying them in your writing.

1. Choose one or more journal articles or books in your field of study, recognized as authoritative, valid sources.

2. During 10 minutes of your practice session, begin to read slowly one article identifying the technical terms you are not familiar with and the terms you *think* you know but aren't quite sure about. Use your timer so you won't go over the 10-minute mark.

3. During the last 10 minutes place each term in your personal glossary (it can be in a word processor or one of those little phonebooks I mentioned). For each term, check how the authors defined it in the article from which you drew the term and copy that definition (with the source/reference). If the article doesn't define it, make a note to yourself to look for the definition, then add it to your glossary during tomorrow's writing session.

Example

Some time ago, I wrote a systematic literature review focusing on the relationships among self-esteem, adolescents' sexual attitudes, intentions, and behaviors. As I noted in Chapter 2, when I began writing that paper I realized my understanding of the construct *self-esteem* was rather shaky. I decided, then, to develop my own self-esteem glossary. One entry dealt with the number of dimensions contained in self-esteem. In the table below you can see what I came up with based on my readings. As you will note, I wrote down what I found, often verbatim, but also added personal comments or notes. Even today, in my research, I still refer to this little glossary whenever I'm dealing with the construct *self-esteem*. Developing the glossary helped me gain depth in understanding the concept, a depth I had previously lacked. It was well worth the time invested in it.

Multidimensionality of the concept *Self-Esteem*	Global x Specific	Rosenberg et al. (1995). Global self-esteem and specific self-esteem: different concepts, different outcomes: Global → psychological wellbeing; Specific → Behavior "Insofar as this facet relates to some area of competence, specific self-esteem has much in common with the concept of self-efficacy" (p. 144—refers to Bandura, 1982). This study was the first to have compared the predictability of global x specific self-esteem for behavioral outcomes and psychological well-being (p. 146). *American Sociological Review,* 60(1): 141–156. According to Kohn, Alfie (1994). The truth about self-esteem. *Phi Delta Kappan,* 76(4): "Unfortunately, what most of us have in mind when we use the term—and when we try to devise programs to enhance children's self-esteem—is the broadest version of the concept, which also appears to be the least valuable" (referring to global self-esteem). "There is also no agreement about whether SE/SC is best conceptualized in unidimensional, multidimensional, or hierarchical terms" (Haney & Durlak, 1998, p. 424). "One limitation of Rosenberg's extensive research is that it treats self-esteem as a global and unidimensional variable" (Gecas, p. 9).

NOTE: Keep in mind that every field of knowledge has its own technical dictionary and thesaurus (more on these tools in Exercise 24). Make it a point to own the best ones in your field. Refer to them when building your own glossary. You will find these resources very useful as you create your own, more specialized, and in-depth glossary.

Electronic Sources

Dictionary.com: http://dictionary.reference.com/browse/glossary
Oxford Dictionaries: http://www.oxforddictionaries.com
Roget's Thesaurus of English Words and Phrases: http://poets.notredame.ac.jp/
  Roget/
Visual Thesaurus: http://www.visualthesaurus.com
Vocab Vitamins: http://www.vocabvitamins.com

References

Alves, R. A. (1979). *Protestantismo e repressão*. São Paulo, SP: Editora Atica.

Boice, R. (1997). Which is more productive, writing in binge patterns of creative illness or in moderation? *Written Communication, 14*(4), 435–459.

Goodson, P. (2010). *Theory in health promotion research and practice: Thinking outside the box*. Sudbury, MA: Jones & Bartlett.

Minkler, M. (1997). Introduction and overview. In M. Minkler (Ed.), *Community organizing & community building for health* (pp. 3–19). New Brunswick, NJ: Rutgers University Press.

Minkler, M., & Wallerstein, N. (1997). Improving health through community organization and community building: A health education perspective. In M. Minkler (Ed.), *Community organizing & community building for health* (pp. 30–52). New Brunswick, NJ: Rutgers University Press.

Oxford Desk Dictionary and Thesaurus (American ed.). (1997). New York: Berkley Books; Oxford University Press.

Payack, P. J. J. (2008). *A million words and counting: How global English is rewriting the world*. New York: Citadel Press Books.

Smith, B., & Sparkes, A. C. (2005). Men, sport, spinal cord injury, and narratives of hope. *Social Science & Medicine, 61*, 1095–1105.

Thompson, B. (2006). *Foundations of behavioral statistics: An insight-based approach*. New York: Guilford Press.

Chapter Four

Polish the Grammar

Summary

Think About It . . .

EXERCISE 12—Learn From the Masters

EXERCISE 13—Identify Patterns of Problems

EXERCISE 14—Practice Grammar Rules

EXERCISE 15—Copy

A writer who can't write in a grammarly manner better shut up shop.

Artemus Ward (1834–1867)

Think About It . . .

Most people *hate* grammar. Yet speakers of all languages—despite their feelings—are considered grammar experts by language scientists. Native speakers of any idiom have what is often referred to as a subconscious knowledge, or an implicit competence, when it comes to the language they learned in childhood. Whether you hate it or love it, you're a grammar expert, at least in your native language.

But what *is* grammar, after all? The answer to this simple question can be quite complex and, as with everything else in academic life, will vary according to whom you ask.

Most nonlinguists will answer that grammar is a compilation of the rules native speakers are expected to follow when speaking or writing a given language. But even the people who insist on this point of view about grammar will admit, along with Peter Elbow and Pat Belanoff (1995), that "language is a matter of social negotiation, and 'rules' about what is correct are slowly but constantly shifting like the coastline" (p. 528).

But ask a linguist the question, "What is grammar?" and he/she will respond by saying grammar is more than a set of rules. Grammar describes the principles or strategies used by native speakers to communicate. For linguists, grammar is the *theory* of the language. Grammar tells the story of how a particular language behaves in practice. It explains which strategies people use when they utter a sentence, ask a question, or describe what someone else has said or done. It explains the mechanisms through which plurals are formed, passing time is captured in words, and writing is coded for silences, stops, or tone.

If we accept as valid the answers from both groups (nonlinguists and linguists), we can understand grammar as having two functions: prescriptive and descriptive. Grammar can both dictate how to use words or sentences correctly (prescriptive) and tell us how a certain language works (descriptive; Schmitt, 2002).

From a learner's perspective, dealing with descriptive grammar is much more interesting than memorizing prescriptive grammar rules. Why? First, because when explaining how a language works, descriptive grammar is not concerned with right or wrong but merely with how communication occurs. Descriptive grammar does not require one to memorize rules of correct speech. I remember learning about generative grammar—one type of descriptive grammar—while studying for my bachelor's degree in linguistics. From Day 1, my professors repeatedly emphasized the mantra, "There is no right or wrong here!"

Second, descriptive grammar is more interesting because, in an indirect but fascinating way, understanding a language's grammatical structure allows insights into that language's worldview. For instance, consider languages that attribute gender to inanimate objects or phenomena; compare them to languages that assign gender only to human beings or animals. Portuguese (one of my two first languages), for instance, attributes gender to objects such as tables (feminine), cars (masculine), the sun (masculine), as well as to abstract phenomena such as emotions (feminine) and perceptions (feminine). There is no gender-neutral category or anything equivalent to the English pronoun *it*. English, on the other hand, does not attribute gender to objects or phenomena but does contain the neutral gender category (*it*), also used for animals, children, infants, babies, and fetuses. Such a feature raises the question, "What could this *mean?*" What cultural elements lead one language to emphasize genderization and lead another language to deemphasize it and create a gender-neutral category? (I know, I know; *genderization* is not a word . . .) Interesting questions such as these are often spurred by the study of grammar—but we wouldn't know it, would we, given the far-from-interesting manner in which our grammar teachers drilled us in school.

Here's the take-home message: The world of grammar is much larger and more fascinating than what we were taught. It extends far beyond dull rules to encompass understanding a language's entire structure and behavior. Think of it this way: Languages are complex adaptive systems; grammar studies these complex systems. The study of grammar, therefore, is akin to the study of chaos or dynamic systems theories (Larsen-Freeman, 1997). That's why studying grammar can be (and often is) extremely complex—but always intriguing!

I'm sure you've noticed academic writing has a grammar of its own. Academic writing in English behaves almost as a dialect—a second English, if you will. Academinglish is much like all the recently emerging -*lishes*, such as Chinglish, Hinglish, and Spanglish (Payack, 2008). Academic authors must master the complex structure and rules the dialect contains. In this sense, mastering academic writing in English is almost akin to mastering English as a second language (ESL). Here, native English speakers and ESL writers are more or less at the same level: They both have to face a learning curve when it comes to their academic writing.

Unfortunately, many writers approach learning academic English simply as the task of acquiring rules: Obey the rules and academic writing will follow naturally. Not so. Mastering the academic dialect involves more than merely memorizing rules such as "Always provide citations when writing about facts or data," or "Write in an impersonal voice, using third person; avoid using *I* or *We*." Mastering the *tone* of academic writing (formal but not stuffy), adapting to different audiences (math teachers versus mathematicians), and structuring the various presentation formats (term paper, journal article, technical report, grant proposal) are also requirements of academic writing. More often than not, the rules governing these requirements are fuzzy and not explicit, but they exist. Ignoring them can be costly.

The remainder of this book will help you gain mastery over several of these requirements as you practice your academic writing. In this section, however, we'll focus on developing better grammar as it relates specifically to syntax rules and English language usage. Don't

Research Shows . . .

Michael C. Mayrath (2008) studied "top-producing" authors publishing in the field of educational psychology. The main research question was, "Why are these authors so productive?" Analyzing the interview data he obtained, Mayrath uncovered four factors these authors claimed were responsible for their success:

- Collaboration
- Passion/curiosity
- Research skills
- Time management

Of special interest is this portion in Mayrath's report:

Almost all authors I surveyed mentioned the need to schedule time to write. Karen Harris said she was taught a "calendar trick by a very productive researcher" when she was an assistant professor. The trick is that "research and writing time belong on your calendar." . . . Andrew Elliot responded similarly, "At least half of each working day I completely isolate myself from all distractions, and this helps me to get things accomplished." (p. 52)

fret: I won't recommend you go back to your high school grammar books, or go take another grammar course if you're an ESL writer. The exercises I present in this chapter emphasize a more practical approach, one that is stress-free and results in lifelong, sustained learning. With time, you may even learn to *love* grammar!

EXERCISE 12—LEARN FROM THE MASTERS

TIME NEEDED: 15 minutes x session

MATERIALS NEEDED: Timer; book (or other media) about writing well, grammar, or punctuation

---

This week's exercise is simple:

1. Choose a book (or any other media) focused on good-quality writing, grammar, or punctuation. I list several useful sources in the Appendix. There are also many good websites and recordings regarding quality writing, but for this exercise I focus on using a book, just because . . . well, that's what I most like to use. I'm a book person. What can I say?

2. Read your chosen book for 15 minutes, before beginning your writing session for the day. Most books will teach you different aspects of correctness or formality, which you can apply immediately in your writing. Remember not to exceed your 15 minutes so you're not using reading about writing as an excuse for not writing. A few pages a day (even one) will really add up if you keep reading on a daily basis. Trust me on this one. I have read many, many books by tackling only two or three pages a day—books I would not have read had I waited for big chunks of reading time (sound familiar?).

3. Apply what you learned from your reading in the day's writing session. As you write, pay particular attention to the recommendations made in your reading. As frequently as possible during the writing sessions this week, apply what you have read.

Example

My favorite book—of the kind I recommend above—talks about punctuation. Its title: *Eats, Shoots & Leaves*. I had to ask my friend, when she recommended the book, to repeat the title three times before I could make any sense of it—especially after she mentioned there was a panda drawn on the cover! Lynne Truss authored and published the book in 2003. It is a gem in its ability to grab the reader and not let go.

But how does she manage to engage readers when writing about such a boring topic as punctuation? First, Truss is a captivating and brilliant writer. Second, she crafted the book in such a way, it became not only interesting but outrageously funny! My students have said it's almost embarrassing to read the book in public places such as restaurants or airplanes because the reader can't help but laugh out loud . . . so loud, in fact, it disturbs others.

Yes: the book is hilarious, but it is every bit as instructive as it is witty. Oh, it also allows you to have fun correcting other people's mistakes. The book comes with a page containing punctuation mark stickers you can tag on public signs or your friends' papers. (I gift-wrapped the largest apostrophe on that sheet and gave it to one of my students who couldn't use an apostrophe correctly to save his life! Eventually, he *did* learn how to use it correctly. I may have saved his life!)

Truss (2003) describes the history of punctuation marks in the English language and provides multiple examples of their misuse. It's in the stories about improper usage that the fun—and the learning—begins. In the segment I transcribed below, Truss describes her dismay in witnessing an example of the widespread disregard for correct punctuation. As we read the description, we can't help but learn how to use an apostrophe correctly:

> Everywhere one looks, there are signs of ignorance and indifference. What about that film *Two Weeks Notice*? Guaranteed to give [punctuation] sticklers a very nasty turn, that was—its posters slung along the sides of buses in letters four feet tall, with no apostrophe in sight. I remember, at the start of the *Two Weeks Notice* publicity campaign in the spring of 2003, emerging cheerfully from Victoria Station (was I whistling?) and stopping dead in my tracks with my fingers in my mouth. Where was the apostrophe? Surely there should be an apostrophe on that bus? If it were "one month's notice" there would be an apostrophe (I reasoned); yes, and if it were "one week's notice" there would be an apostrophe. Therefore "two weeks' notice" requires an apostrophe! Buses that I should have caught (the 73; two 38s) sailed off up Buckingham Palace Road while I communed thus at length with my inner stickler, unable to move or, indeed, regain any sense of perspective. (pp. 2–3)

As I read this passage—and learn that *two weeks notice* is incorrect and *two weeks' notice* is the correct form—I'm forced to pay attention to my own writing. I will no longer write *the samples characteristics* when I want to say *the characteristics of the sample*. I will, instead, begin to self-correct and write: *the sample's characteristics*.

Learning about correct writing, in this way, becomes more enjoyable, less stressful, and very productive. Had I recommended you memorize the rules for the appropriate use of possessive apostrophes, you probably would have ignored the suggestion and continued to write *the samples characteristics*, wouldn't you? I probably would have, too!

EXERCISE 13—IDENTIFY PATTERNS OF PROBLEMS

TIME NEEDED: 15 minutes x session

MATERIALS NEEDED: Timer; help from a trusted reader, friend, or colleague

A few years ago, some of my former students surprised me by confessing they felt really disappointed when I returned their papers or manuscript drafts after reviewing them. Here at Texas A&M University, where maroon is the school's official color, a specific phrase reflects one's loyalty to the school: "He/she bleeds maroon!" Unfortunately, my students were also applying that phrase to the feedback they had received from me: generous red markings on each and every page—so many, in fact, they couldn't help but admit their papers bled maroon. "We felt paralyzed; we didn't know where to *begin* making changes," they added as a footnote to their disappointment, careful not to offend or hurt my feelings.

Far from offensive, their remarks led me to rethink how I gave feedback and to look for more helpful ways to edit/revise students' papers. With time and practice, I learned that instead of marking each awkward phrase, grammar mistake, punctuation, misspelling, or inappropriate transition, my students learned more if I focused on identifying **patterns of problems** in their writing.

When training POWER consultants to assist graduate students with their writing (see Chapter 1 for a description of POWER Services), I coach them to triage students' papers, much the same way an emergency room nurse might triage wounded patients: What is the most pressing, urgent, critical problem here? Fortunately, a grid containing only four patterns can be used to diagnose the most salient problems in one's writing. Writers (in English) tend to exhibit one of these four difficulties as their *main problem:* (1) lack of clarity, (2) faulty organization, (3) incorrect grammar, or (4) inappropriate usage.

As an example, let's pretend your most pressing problem is incorrect grammar. Discovering your *patterns of problems with grammar*—in other words, which mistakes you tend to repeat consistently—and learning how to correct these will provide important strategies to improve your writing. As you begin to make these corrections, you internalize the correct forms and stop making those mistakes, even in your early, messy drafts!

Therefore, for this exercise you need to do the following:

1. Identify someone who will read one or two pages of your writing. Don't ask anyone to read an entire 30-page paper right now, only a couple of pages.

2. Ask this person to read your piece (preferably, to read it *with you*, out loud) and identify what seems to be the most dominant grammar problem, the mistake you make most often grammarwise.

3. Ask this person for suggestions on how to improve that particular issue, how to correct it. If appropriate, ask for some reference materials you might consult (e.g., a grammar manual, a helpful website, or someone else's input).

4. Take notes of this feedback. If your reader doesn't have a suggestion for correcting the problem, try, at least, to identify what the problem *is*. Then, consult a grammar manual, a website, or ask someone else for help.

5. Return to your writing and focus on correcting/editing only that one, repeated mistake you identified with your reader. This is not the time to worry about correcting *everything*.

6. After you have corrected Problem No. 1 throughout your draft, you should return to your reader. Ask him/her to check whether your corrections were appropriate and ask him/her to identify the *next* salient problem (Problem No. 2).

7. Repeat steps 5 and 6 and identify Problem No. 3.

8. The principle behind the exercise is this: Avoid trying to catch or correct *everything* that might be wrong in your writing. Focus on one problem at a time. Identify the mistake, correct it. Look for the same or similar mistakes in other parts of your project. Correct them. Only through this catching-and-correcting process will you internalize the grammar rule without having to recall or think about it each time you write.

EXERCISE 14—PRACTICE GRAMMAR RULES

TIME NEEDED: 15 minutes x session

MATERIALS NEEDED: Timer; a book on English grammar for academic writers

Even if grammar is not your main problem, you certainly can improve your writing by paying attention to and refining your application of grammar rules. Brushing up on grammar skills through practice (notice I said *practice*, not *memory*) can only improve your writing, whether you are an ESL writer or a native English writer.

For this exercise you will do the following:

1. Choose an English grammar book or website (I provide some suggestions in the Appendix).

2. Focus on one rule the book/website describes per writing session.

3. Read and understand the rule.

4. Apply that rule during the subsequent writing session, at least once.

5. Even better: When you apply the rule, write about it. Make a note to yourself (either in your text or in your writing journal) regarding *how* you applied the rule. Writing about how you applied something—not just applying it—adds a level of depth to your learning, inaccessible otherwise. Here's an example of what I'm talking about. In *A Community of Writers*, coauthor Peter Elbow talks about editing a portion of his writing. He discusses editing an informal text, trying to make it more formal. Here are his notes, explaining what he did:

> When I looked for informal or personal elements to remove I came up with these: contractions; dashes as punctuation; sentences without a verb; conversational words like "till" and "bit"; conversational expressions like "just have to choose" (changed to "simply have to choose"). (Elbow & Belanoff, 1995, p. 529)

Try to emulate this practice: Write about your writing and editing processes, especially when you're focused on learning one specific rule. Say something like,

> I've used the article *the* in this sentence because the noun *game* referred to one specific game, the game I watched last night. The new sentence reads: "My friends and I watched *the* last World Cup soccer game last night" (instead of my original, "My friends and I watched last World Cup soccer game last night").

Tip for ESL Writers

Most word processors have a built-in grammar checker. It can be a helpful tool for catching grammatical errors but lacks the ability to teach us what is wrong within our writing (and why it is wrong). At times, it will also highlight errors that aren't really mistakes but merely unique writing styles.

The Internet provides many resources related to grammar checking that can be more helpful because they actually teach us what we're doing wrong. One example is www.grammarly.com. You can use its free (but more limited) service by copying and pasting a portion of your text onto the website, or you can register (for a fee) for the complete package. The paid services also include checking for plagiarism, to see if your text is unique or if it is too similar to other people's writings.

I don't have any connection with or interest in promoting this particular website; I mention it as an example of what is available on the Internet. I've tried the free service and liked how it explained my mistakes, and enjoyed that I learned something while using it.

Regardless of what helpful sources you utilize, always bear this in mind: (a) These sources will not write for you, and (b) these sources are not *perfect*. They make their own mistakes while detecting ours. Therefore, don't rely on them exclusively. Always get feedback from your colleagues, professors, and friends.

EXERCISE 15—COPY

TIME NEEDED: 15 minutes x session

MATERIALS NEEDED: Timer; a model journal article (or other piece of academic writing)

Did you have mixed feelings when you read the word *copy* in the title above? Did it cross your mind—even for a nanosecond—I might be suggesting you plagiarize somebody else's writing? Rest assured, I am not asking you to do anything of the sort. The focus here is on presenting a strategy useful especially for ESL writers.

From my ESL students I often hear the following comment: "Dr. Goodson, I *read* a lot in English; I read many, many articles and books before writing, but I am not able to *write* in English as well as English speakers write." I know these students do, in fact, read quite a lot but, somehow, the reading does not translate into better writing. This is an interesting paradox, given most writing instructors highly recommend reading good writing as *essential* for improving one's own skills!

After repeatedly coming across this theme of *reading a lot,* I began wondering if the problem lay in the difference between the two behaviors: Reading and writing are different neuromotor tasks. When activated, they draw on different mechanisms in our brains. Because reading and writing, from the perspective of our brains and our hands, constitute such different actions, it is *not* reasonable to expect that repeatedly performing one task will automatically facilitate the other: Reading more doesn't necessarily translate into writing more, or into writing better.

As I mentioned above, many accomplished authors strongly recommend *reading* as something all writers must do because it informs their writing and makes them better writers. The mechanism at play in reading good literature for writing better is this: Reading good literature or well-written articles (or grant proposals or books) exposes us to good writing, places us in the company of people we would like to emulate. Yet, being in good company and listening attentively to what other authors have to say will not automatically change our writing. Human behavior is far more complex than the monkey-see-monkey-do behavior of chimps. It is precisely *this complexity* that does not allow us to become Pulitzer Prize winners just because we read only works written by Pulitzer Prize–winning authors.

So . . . if *reading* good writing does not transfer into writing well, will *writing* good writing work? Many researchers and writers seem to think so.

For example, William Zinsser (1988)—an extraordinary writer in his own right and a former writing professor at Yale University—wrote in *Writing to Learn*, "Writing is learned through imitation" (p. 15).

Daphne Gray-Grant (2008)—author and owner of the successful Publication Coach website—also remarks, in one lesson in her writing course:

> I also encourage you to **copy writers you like**—a trick I learned by reading about Benjamin Franklin. He looked for writers he really admired and then took a few pages of their work and copied them in longhand. (You can use your computer if you prefer!) Of course, he never attempted to pass this work off as his own. The purpose of the exercise was simply to better (and more deeply) understand how other writers achieve what they do. Try it![1]

Another validation that copying may improve one's writing comes from studies of outstanding performers (Olympic athletes, world chess champions, famous musicians, among others). Remember Daniel Coyle's (2009) *The Talent Code*, mentioned in Chapter 1? In the book, Coyle refers to imitation as an element common among most peak performers. One example he gives centers on an 8-year-old girl who, at the time he wrote the book, was "one of the top-ranked age-group [tennis] players in the country" (p. 80). She had a rather unique style of hitting backhands, quite similar to another famous player's. Upon further investigation, Coyle learned the girl's entire family revered this famous tennis player and *routinely* watched his videotaped games. Coyle writes,

> Carolyn in particular watched [the videotapes of the games] whenever she could. In other words, in her short life she had seen Roger Federer hit a backhand tens of thousands of times. She had watched the backhand and, without knowing, simply absorbed the essence of it. (p. 81)

As Coyle notes in this quote, merely *watching* the expert player didn't shape this girl's talent, but *imitating* his technique, embodying what she observed, did.

The principle, here, is this: Copying good-quality writing, as a form of practicing good writing technique, can lead to better writing. Unfortunately, because we fear being accused of plagiarism, we have been conditioned to stay away from this strategy. If we could get used to copying as a *practice* strategy and distinguish the copying practice from plagiarizing, we would be tapping into a rich technique for improving our writing.

So, here's the exercise:

1. Set your timer for 15 minutes.

2. Choose a published article or book chapter in your field that you (or your colleagues or professors) consider well written. If possible, choose something written by an authority.

3. With that writing piece in hand, begin to copy its first paragraph. BUT, here's the trick: Copy very, very, very s-l-o-w-l-y. Some people may prefer to do this longhand, instead of using the computer. The reason for slowing down? You pay much more attention to what you're doing than if you're writing at normal speed.

4. Copy one paragraph in each writing session (copying may take less than your timed 15 minutes, and that's not a problem). The key to productive practice, however, is this: It must be done s-l-o-w-l-y. You may do just one short paragraph each session.

   If you're worried about plagiarism, don't be; you are merely doing an exercise, much like practicing scales on the piano or hitting a tennis ball for the first time. You are **not going to use these words as your own** in your writing (that's what plagiarism is: using other people's words as your own, without acknowledging they are not yours). When you *do* include in your work words similar to the ones you copied, you must obey the proper citation and paraphrasing rules.

5. As you are copying, try not to focus your attention too much on *what* you are copying. Don't think about the content. Try to let your hands and brain become familiar with certain ways of saying things, with certain prepositions after certain verbs, with different choices of words. DO NOT ATTEMPT TO MEMORIZE anything. The exercise aims at familiarizing your brain with a certain style of writing. The goal is familiarity, not retention or recall. For example, after practicing for a while, whenever you type the word *familiar* your brain and your hands will want to write the word *with* immediately after *familiar*. Why? Because you've copied/written the phrase *familiar with* so many times before. Zinsser (1988) describes it this way: "Nobody will write well unless he gets **into his ear and into his metabolism** a sense of how the language works and what it can be made to do" (p. 15; emphasis added). As you slowly proceed with copying, try to remember: You're getting the writing into your metabolism. Chew slowly.

6. After you're done, observe the paragraph you copied and ask yourself these questions:

   • How did the author structure the paragraph? How did he/she *start* the paragraph? How did the paragraph *end?*
   • Was this a well-built paragraph? (See Exercise 21 to learn what makes a well-built paragraph.)
   • How did the author connect *this* paragraph to the previous one?

- What does each sentence look like? Did the author use passive or active voice? Is the sentence short and to the point, or long and convoluted?
- What technical or academic words did the author use? (You may want to add some of these words to your personal specialized glossary—see Exercise 11.)

7. After coming up with answers for these and similar questions you may have, step away from the exercise and begin your daily writing session. In your writing, try to use what you learned when copying the paragraph: Experiment with using similar techniques.

Several of my ESL students have been practicing copying as part of their daily writing sessions. They have all reported success, so far. They also have consistently emphasized that slowing down during the copying allows them to see things in other authors' writings they cannot see when merely reading.

Note

1. Excerpt from Lesson 3 of Gray-Grant's Extreme Writing Makeover, a subscription-based writing course, accessed September 24, 2010 (http://publication-coach.com/Extreme_Writing_Makeover.php).

Electronic Sources

Grammarly: www.grammarly.com
Publication Coach: http://publicationcoach.com

References

Coyle, D. (2009). *The talent code: Greatness isn't born. It's grown. Here's how.* New York: Bantam Dell.

Elbow, P., & Belanoff, P. (1995). *A community of writers: A workshop course in writing* (2nd ed.). New York: McGraw-Hill.

Gray-Grant, D. (2008). *8 1/2 steps to writing faster, better.* Vancouver, BC: Highbury Street Books.

Larsen-Freeman, D. (1997). Chaos/complexity science and second language acquisition. *Applied Linguistics, 18*(2), 141–165.

Mayrath, M. (2008). Attributions of productive authors in educational psychology journals. *Educational Psychology Review, 20,* 41–56.

Payack, P. J. J. (2008). *A million words and counting: How global English is rewriting the world*. New York: Citadel Press Books.

Schmitt, N. (Ed.). (2002). *An introduction to applied linguistics*. London: Hodder Education.

Truss, L. (2003). *Eats, shoots & leaves: The zero tolerance approach to punctuation*. New York: Gotham Books.

Zinsser, W. (1988). *Writing to learn: How to write—and think—clearly about any subject at all*. New York: Harper & Row.

Chapter Five

Get Feedback

I much prefer a compliment, insincere or not, to sincere criticism.

Titus Maccius Plautus (254–184 B.C.)

Think About It . . .

On a scale of 1 to 10, where 1 represents *can't think of anything more painful* and 10 is *just love it!*, how would you rate your experience with getting feedback on your writing? If you have just started your academic writing career, chances are you haven't yet made friends with getting feedback. If you are a seasoned academic, you most likely feel more comfortable receiving it because you have learned over time that feedback *usually* tends to improve your writing and, therefore, is worth the trouble to ask for.

Yet most of us—novices or seasoned authors—seek feedback much as we buy bitter vegetables at the grocery store: We know they're good for us, but we don't particularly crave them. Admit it: You're not writing whatever it is you're writing and thinking, "Oh, I can't *wait* to finish this section so I can get some feedback on it!"

So why do we have such a love/hate relationship with feedback? Depending on our personalities and prior experiences, the answer can be complex. Curiously, though, the root of the problem is rather plain: We haven't learned much *about* feedback itself, how to ask for it effectively, or how to make feedback work for us.

For a moment, try to remember: What responses to your writing efforts did you receive in grade school, in college, or in graduate school? Most of my students report their feedback experiences as ranging from mildly negative to intensely traumatic. Personally, I can't recall any terrifying feedback moments, but I do remember *hating it* when someone suggested perhaps I could rewrite portions of my text to make it . . . hum . . . *better. Better?!?!?!?! It's nearly perfect, already! That section alone took almost 10 hours to write! What are they talking about?* You get the picture: I dreaded hearing I should rewrite something that had already taken so much of my time, so much work.

Gradually, however, I learned to value useful feedback. Notice I said *useful* (not every piece of feedback improves your text—we'll get to this point a bit later). But it wasn't until I read what Peter Elbow had to say about feedback that I *truly* began to value readers' reactions. Now I'm so hooked on feedback, I can't wait to finish a piece of writing in order to see what readers will have to say about it (okay, it's weird, I know . . .).

So . . . what constitutes *useful feedback,* after all? Here's where Peter Elbow's (1998; Elbow & Belanoff, 1995) work has helped me: He talks about *different kinds* of feedback being useful at *different stages* of writing. Useful feedback is the feedback that helps move the writing from one stage to another: from the maturing-the-initial-idea stage through the more-or-less-complete rough draft to the final, polished version. Feedback is useful when it is suitable for a particular stage in the writing process.

To this fundamental notion that authors need different feedback at different moments, Elbow adds another important element. He proposes that most of us learn to dread feedback because nearly all the input we have ever received has been of one kind only: *evaluative.* In other words, so far during our writing lives we have been writing for teachers, professors, peer reviewers, and editors. Given the nature of their jobs, the only feedback we get from them is evaluation of our work's *quality,* with the chief purpose of highlighting its *weaknesses.* My first step toward valuing feedback was to learn there are *different types of useful* feedback, many of which are *not* critical or evaluative.

I also have learned evaluative feedback is *especially useless* in a writing project's beginning stages. For instance, if I'm struggling to write about something new to me, something I have no idea how to introduce, how to make interesting, or how to argue intelligently, the feedback I need at this early stage should come from someone who can say: "Yes, the idea here, in this paragraph, sounds interesting. This other idea, in this other paragraph, sounds boring; nothing new. Perhaps if you go with that first idea, add this aspect, or another dimension, you would have something really interesting!"

See? *This* kind of feedback, in the first moments of my writing project can be immensely

Research Shows . . .

Claire M. Rickard and colleagues (2009) investigated what effect a structured writing course combined with a writing group might have—over a 2-year period—on the publication rates of academics in various disciplines at the Monash University School of Rural Health in Victoria, Australia. The course lasted 5 days, with lectures, discussions, writing, and feedback from consultants. The support group met once a month for 4 hours. Most participants were at the assistant professor or research assistant level.

According to the study's authors, "Two year pre and post submissions increased from 9 to 33 articles in peer-reviewed journals. Those who attended more than 10 support meetings submitted an average 5.4 manuscripts in the two year follow-up period, compared with an average of 1.2 papers for those who attended less than 10 meetings. Overall, publications (in print) per person increased from a baseline of 0.5 to 1.2 per year" (p. 517).

valuable and can help, in fact, shape the entire piece. At such early stages—when I haven't even generated enough text to consider it a piece of writing, evaluative feedback does not help: Telling me the only two paragraphs I wrote don't connect, my paragraphs are not tightly developed, the word *idea* is misspelled, and paragraph two has a long compound sentence, really, really DOES NOT HELP!!! But saying the idea sounds good and it's worth pursuing, *that* is the kind of useful feedback I need at that moment. It will help me generate more text and move my project forward.

And as I continue writing, there will be times when the most useful feedback someone can give will simply be to point to unclear portions, or to ideas that do not flow smoothly. However, even at this stage, where I have written a nice chunk of text, *evaluative* feedback may not be the most useful.

To fully grasp the notion of *different kinds of feedback being useful at different stages in the writing process,* let's practice receiving these different types using the exercises in this chapter.

Types of Feedback

Peter Elbow (1998, p. 240) distinguishes between criterion-based feedback and reader-based feedback in *Writing With Power.* Criterion-based feedback is evaluative and represents the type of feedback we received the most in school. The criteria may vary, but, essentially, this feedback looks for answers to questions such as these:

a. What is the quality of the content of the writing: the ideas, the perceptions, the point of view?

b. How well is the writing organized?

c. How effective is the language?

d. Are there mistakes or inappropriate choices in usage?

Reader-based feedback, conversely, isn't concerned with whether the writing meets standards of clarity, organization, or usage. It is concerned with how the writing *impacts the reader.* Peter Elbow (1998, p. 240) offers these questions, among others listed in his book, to elicit reader-based feedback:

a. What was happening to you, moment by moment, as you were reading the piece of writing?

b. Summarize the writing: give your understanding of what it says or what happened in it.

c. Make up some images for the writing and the transaction it creates with you.

To these two types of feedback—criterion and reader based—I would add a third one: content-based feedback. This feedback focuses exclusively on the accuracy of the content and of the arguments. It assesses how well your piece relates to the available information in the field, how much value it adds to the literature, and how adequately you presented the arguments or supporting evidence. To elicit content-based feedback, you need to ask your reader:

a. How do I see this piece fitting into the current literature in our field?

b. Does my writing make a contribution to the field? Does it add anything new?

c. Do I fail to address any important issues? Do I neglect references to important studies or theories?

d. Are my analyses correct? Are they appropriate for the data and the questions I have raised?

The exercises in this chapter will help you practice obtaining reader-, criterion-, and content-based feedback. They also will help you *value* feedback as a way to improve your writing *quality*. They will help you focus on, and develop a strategy for, obtaining the most useful feedback at different stages of your writing.

But I must forewarn you, as does Tara Gray (2005) in her book *Publish & Flourish:* "Getting help from your readers is going to take a high proportion of your time as a writer, and you need to *plan for this* and start early" (p. 57; emphasis added).

So . . . let's start!

EXERCISE 16—GET FEEDBACK ON EARLY DRAFTS

TIME NEEDED: Varies from 05 to 60 minutes

MATERIALS NEEDED: Early drafts of your writing project

Getting feedback on early drafts is scariest because these tend to be the worst-quality drafts authors generate (yes, all authors!). But getting feedback at this stage is extremely useful, for you may receive suggestions that help shape, structure, or otherwise package the information you are presenting.

Early drafts should be shown only to people whom you trust, people who are also willing to share *their* early drafts with you. Easier said than done, of course. Very few authors are eager to share with anyone what writer Anne Lamott (1994) calls "shitty first drafts." But these early drafts are *necessary* for producing the final, polished piece. As Lamott explains it:

> Now, practically even better news than that of short assignments is the idea of shitty first drafts. All good writers write them. This is how they end up with good second drafts, and terrific third drafts. . . . For me and most of the other writers I know, writing is not rapturous. In fact, the only way I can get anything written at all is to write really, really shitty first drafts. (pp. 21–22)

Shitty first drafts, then, are *required* for getting to good final drafts. You *need* them. They are a fact of your writing life. Just accept the fact and write them!

Okay, so you produce your shitty first draft and summon the courage to share it. Now what? With whom should you share it? What kind of help do you need at this stage?

Tara Gray (2005) recommends sharing early drafts with *non-experts*. She defines non-experts as people who have two characteristics: They do not hold a terminal degree in your field, and they are "people you have absolutely no need to impress" (p. 57). Colleagues you trust implicitly, close friends, or even supportive family members can function well as early draft, non-expert readers.

Because these readers don't know your field, they require clearer and more detailed explanations of your topic than the experts do. As you attend to non-experts' need for clearer explanations, detailed examples, or simple definitions, the experts who later read your final drafts will thank you for the clarity you bring to the text. You might want to turn around and thank your non-expert readers because you probably wouldn't have seen the need or cared to struggle for such clarity were it not for their input.

Once you've identified one or two people you trust enough to see your first drafts, what kind of feedback should you ask for? At this stage, obtain reader-based feedback. Remember: You obtain reader-based feedback by asking readers to share what went on in their minds while reading your piece; how they reacted to your writing; how it touched them (or not). This is not the kind of feedback that asks the reader to detect poor writing, or to evaluate the text's quality. According to Elbow (1998), reader-based feedback has the added bonus of keeping you *in control* of your writing. Here's how he explains it:

> Reader-based feedback has the advantage of keeping you more in charge of the whole feedback process. Readers get to tell you what they saw and what happened in them, but *you* take over from there. . . . You get to decide what their reactions mean and what changes if any you want to make. One of the main reasons so many people hate feedback or fail to learn from it is that it makes them feel so helpless. Getting feedback has always felt like putting themselves entirely into someone else's power. You don't do that if you use reader-based feedback. (pp. 246–247)

So here's your exercise for this week:

1. During the first exercise session, brainstorm a list of people with whom you feel comfortable sharing even your worst first drafts and from whom you can obtain honest reader-based feedback. Don't worry about generating a long list. Aim for at least *one name* at this time.

2. Contact the people on your list and ask for their help.

3. If possible, schedule a date/time on your planner when you will meet with your chosen people, or a time when you will send them your initial drafts for feedback.

4. Once your time for meeting (or sending draft materials) is set, keep that time. Honor the appointment as you would honor your own scheduled writing sessions.

5. When asking for feedback on early drafts, remember to say to your reader and ask him/her:

   "This is just a first draft—not yet developed, not very good yet. I need your help to see this piece from a reader's perspective. Right now, I don't need an evaluation of the quality of the writing: I already know it's pretty *bad*, and I will work on improving it later. What I *do need* is for you to read this and tell me:

- What do you think of the idea? Do you think it will work for the purpose or the audience I have in mind?
- When reading this piece, what else comes to mind? What do you remember or think about, as you read it?
- How could I improve? Do you have any suggestions for another approach, a different angle, a more sophisticated argument?
- What sticks in your mind after you finish reading this? What jumps out at you from this piece?"

6. In the remaining practice sessions during the week, write your thoughts about this process, your experience with getting this type of feedback. Reflect on what you have learned. Brainstorm how you might do it differently next time. Keep your writing to no more than 5 minutes each time.

7. Make sure you incorporate the suggested changes into your writing project, if you find them appropriate and useful, during regular writing sessions.

EXERCISE 17—GET FEEDBACK ON MIDDLE DRAFTS

TIME NEEDED: Varies from 05 to 60 minutes

MATERIALS NEEDED: Middle drafts of your writing project

At this point, you may not have had time to move your early draft into the middle-draft stage yet, so you may not be ready to practice this exercise. If so, just read through this exercise and the next one to get a sense of what you will be doing at upcoming stages. You may, then, choose to work on other exercises in the book (skip to Exercise 19 or 20, for instance) and return to this one when your project has advanced.

After you've obtained feedback on your early drafts and reworked those enough so they no longer appear to be "shitty first drafts," it's time to get another type of feedback. Now you need a combination of reader- and criterion-based feedback. Reader-based feedback at this stage, as with early drafts, provides input regarding *what* is being said—and how it impacts the reader. Criterion-based feedback will provide input regarding *how* you're saying it—as well as what needs to change to improve communication.

Your best bet, therefore, is to ask one (or more) *peers* to provide this middle-range feedback. If you are a student, your peers are the kind of readers who know just enough about the topic to anticipate the questions other readers might ask; they know enough to be able to identify the places where the text could be clearer and point out instances where the text flow breaks down. They are middle-range experts.

If you are faculty, your peers might be expert readers, so you may want to save them for the expert-level type of feedback on your *final* drafts (in Exercise 18). I find it very helpful to have my graduate students function as my middle-draft readers: They are excellent at anticipating questions and quick at catching unclear wording.

The exercise for this week, then, is similar to Exercise 16 (on feedback for early drafts):

1. During the first exercise session, brainstorm a list of people with whom you would feel comfortable sharing your middle drafts and from whom you can obtain both reader-based and criterion-based feedback.

2. Contact the people on your list and ask for their help.

3. If possible, schedule a date/time on your planner when you will meet with your chosen people, or a time when you will send them your middle drafts for feedback.

4. Once your time for meeting (or sending draft materials) is set, honor that time.

5. When asking for feedback on middle drafts, remember to say to your reader and ask him/her:

"This is still a draft—not polished yet. I need your help to see this piece from the perspective of a reader in our field. At this moment, I need you to please read this and tell me:

- What do you learn from reading this piece? What impressed you the most?
- How interested will readers in our field be in this article/chapter?
- Are there places where you stumble in the reading? Sentences you need to read more than once to grasp the meaning?
- Does the text flow coherently?
- Can you think of something (an author or a citation, for instance) I am missing or forgetting to include?"

6. During the remaining exercise sessions this week, write your thoughts about this process to see what you have learned and how you might do it differently next time. Keep this writing to no more than 5 minutes each session.

7. Make sure you incorporate the suggested changes, if you find them appropriate and useful, into your project during regular writing sessions. Remember: You're moving toward the final draft. These are your last opportunities to make changes before you submit your piece to the experts (see Exercise 18).

EXERCISE 18—GET FEEDBACK ON FINAL DRAFTS

TIME NEEDED: Varies from 05 to 60 minutes

MATERIALS NEEDED: Final drafts of your writing project

The experts in your field—these include your dissertation or thesis advisor, committee members, faculty colleagues—can provide one of the most useful types of input for your writing: content-related feedback. This feedback is precious, for few people are qualified to provide it. Experts are able to assess both the quality of your writing and your ideas, regarding how well these ideas fit, or conflict, with the current dialogue in your discipline. For this reason alone—the ability to judge your piece's potential contribution—expert readers are like icing on a cake: Their input is the last thing you add to make your piece picture-perfect!

Because only experts can provide this valuable, one-of-a-kind feedback, I recommend graduate students seek all other types of feedback first and save their advisor's feedback for the end. In other words: Don't waste your advisor's time by asking him/her to review your piece while it's still riddled with disorganization, grammar problems, or lack of clarity. Your advisor will be compelled to catch *everything,* every single problem in your writing. Such compulsion to catch everything commonly has two consequences: (a) The advisor gets burned out or exhausted from reading your piece and trying to provide feedback at multiple levels (grammar, punctuation, usage, organization, clarity, and content accuracy, *simultaneously*); and (b) you will receive all the feedback at once, meaning your paper will have more red markings on it than black ink from the original writing! The end result? You will become so overwhelmed you won't know where to start addressing the problems. At least that's what I consistently hear from my graduate students.

Although many professors view my recommendation (actually, Peter Elbow's) as counterintuitive, the attempt to catch all problems at once is simply not a productive strategy. Neither Elbow nor I recommend it. Advisors are able to give the *best* or *most useful* feedback when they can focus on one element exclusively: the content. Content-based feedback already has enough dimensions the advisor needs to be alert to, such as accuracy, scope, and thoroughness. You want the advisor to focus on these dimensions, not be distracted by small grammar mishaps or typos. After all, students are paying their advisors and professors to provide precisely this: high-quality, professional, content-based expertise.

Therefore, in order to maximize the quality of the expert feedback you receive, make sure you have a clean version of the manuscript, preferably one already submitted to several rounds of editing for all other matters (grammar, usage, and punctuation, especially). Let your advisor read for content *only*.

Now, having said this, I need to step back a bit. I realize many advisors and professors actually don't want students to turn in only semifinal or final drafts. They want students to provide evidence the work is being done, step-by-step. Some faculty want to provide input during the entire process. Depending on the student I'm working with, I tend this way myself.

Yet even where the advisor provides input along the way, I still recommend students focus on getting *only* content-related feedback from their advisors. I suggest they say something like this to their professors: "As you read this, please ignore all problems related to grammar, punctuation, usage; I will clean these up later. Where I really need your help is with the *content*: Is it correct? What I wrote, is it accurate? Comprehensive enough? Too detailed?" This frees the professor to focus exclusively on one element and, consequently, provide *better quality* feedback at each step.

If you are faculty, you should seek content-based feedback on your final drafts from expert colleagues or from what author Tara Gray (2005, p. 58) calls "Capital-E Experts." She defines these experts as "the best known scholars in your entire discipline or in the exact area in which you are writing" (p. 56). Gray recommends contacting at least two experts and volunteering to return the favor by reading something of theirs. She also recommends you approach these experts by telling them how *their work* has influenced *your work*. When asking for feedback, also pose specific questions regarding the place of your work within the extant literature and the potential contribution it makes. Remember: These experts can give you feedback *no one else* can give. You want to ask explicitly for *that* specialized feedback and nothing else.

For the exercise this week, then, do the following:

1. During the first exercise session, brainstorm a list of people from whom you wish to obtain expert feedback. If you are a student, the list may include your dissertation/thesis chair or main professor, but try to include other experts as well (other professors or senior colleagues, for instance). If you are faculty, list a few colleagues inside and outside your department/university, as well as a couple of celebrity authors in your field.

2. Contact the people on your list to ask for their help.

3. If possible, schedule a date/time on your planner when you will meet with your chosen people, or a time when you will send them your final draft.

4. Once your time for meeting (or sending draft materials) is set, honor that time.

5. When asking for feedback on final drafts, remember to say to your reader and ask him/her:

   "I've been working on this piece for a while; it's now time to obtain expert feedback. The feedback I need from you is the following:

   • Overall, what do you think of the piece?
   • How do you see this piece fitting in with the current literature in our field?
   • Does my writing make a contribution to the field? Does it add anything new?
   • Do I fail to address any important issues or neglect references to important studies or theories?
   • Where do you recommend I submit for publication?"

6. During the other exercise sessions this week, write your reflections about the process to see what you have learned and how you might do it differently next time. Keep your writing to no more than 5 minutes each session.

7. Make sure you incorporate the suggested changes, if you find them appropriate and useful, into your project during regular writing sessions. Remember: You're polishing a final draft; soon it will be ready to submit for publication (or review). Be sure to pay close attention to every point made by your expert readers!

Tip for ESL Writers

Students who struggle with English grammar and usage should think about having someone read and edit their semifinal drafts before they give them to their dissertation/thesis chair or main professor.

Many universities have writing centers that can assist with editing students' writing. At times, using a professional editor is a good idea also. The expense is reasonable, and it helps the dissertation/thesis chair or the main professor focus exclusively on the content. The professor will not be distracted trying to catch and edit the grammar, usage, or punctuation.

For ESL authors, including faculty who wish to publish in English-language journals, I recommend checking whether the journal's publisher has working agreements with professional editing services. This is now becoming a more common practice, and several journals are partnering with editing services for non-English-speaking authors. Services are not free, but journals often negotiate better prices for their authors.

EXERCISE 19—GET FEEDBACK REGULARLY

TIME NEEDED: Setup: 05 minutes each writing session this week; actual meetings: 60–90 minutes each

MATERIALS NEEDED: Drafts of your writing project

One reason we dread seeking feedback on our writing is that we get it so *rarely*. We don't receive feedback frequently enough to become comfortable with it. Usually, our professors or colleagues see our writing only during its final stages—often only when we turn the paper in for a grade or submit the manuscript for review. And—think about it—many of us turn in or submit a paper only once or twice a semester, sometimes only once or twice a year! In this scheme, it becomes nearly impossible to *get used to* getting feedback; we never have a chance to *practice* receiving and learning from the suggestions we receive.

One way to reduce the stress associated with obtaining and putting feedback to work for you is to get *lots* of it and get it on a *regular basis*. Better yet: Get lots of it on a regular basis from *people you trust*. This strategy allows you to *practice* receiving feedback. Yes, practice: We all need to learn how to ask for feedback and how to deal with it. As you practice obtaining feedback, you will develop a thicker skin—so you're not taking every evaluative comment personally—and you will secure useful, nonevaluative input during *every stage* in your writing process.

The best structure for getting lots of feedback on a regular basis from people you trust is a writing group (aka *writer's group* or *writing circle*). If you don't have a writing group you can readily join, consider starting one. It's not difficult. A writing group can impact your writing as nothing else can. As an added bonus, you have the opportunity to practice *giving feedback,* too. Oftentimes, I'll hear my students say giving feedback is better than receiving, not only because it's less painful but because it's easier to see problems in other people's work, which you do not readily see in your own. Once you see their problems, you tend to ask yourself, "Am I writing like this? Am I making this same mistake?" Such reflection, in itself, can lead to substantial improvements in your writing.

Social support theory claims the strongest predictor of people's well-being is whether they are embedded in a structure of supportive friends, colleagues, contacts, and resource-persons (Glanz, Rimer, & Viswanath, 2008). Developing social support for your writing is the second healthiest step you can take to improve your writing *quality* (the first step is writing regularly).

Alongside support, writing groups also provide a synergy you cannot experience alone. Synergy refers to results obtained from the interaction between two or more agents that yields a combined effect greater than the sum of the individual effects. When two or three people read and assess your work, simultaneously, they feed off one another's comments. The readers begin to brainstorm creative ideas and provide suggestions that, in turn, might lead your writing into entirely new and unexpected directions! This can be especially motivating in the early stages of your writing projects.

See if you can find an academic writing group to join. If you don't have any options to choose from, consider creating your own group. This exercise will help you take the few steps needed to start a writing group of your own:

1. Spend one practice session this week thinking about the type of support and feedback that would benefit you most. Would you rather have less-evaluative, reader-based feedback, or do you want more-critical, criterion-based or evaluative-type feedback? Do you want feedback from people in your field, or would it be okay to get feedback from people in other areas, in order to sense whether your text communicates clearly, despite readers' expertise? Or, perhaps the most important feedback you need at this point is not feedback at all but motivation to stay on track and continue to write on a regular basis. You should give each of these options some thought when deciding who to invite to participate in the group.

2. In the next practice session, brainstorm a list of people who are good candidates for the group, based on the type of feedback they can provide vis-à-vis the type of feedback you wish to obtain routinely. Generate a list with more people than the group will hold, since a few candidates may decline your invitation.

3. Next, contact the people on your list and tell them what you would like to do. Let them know exactly what you're thinking about, what the expectations are, what their job would be. Discuss potential schedules and try to gauge each person's enthusiasm for your idea. If you perceive someone is not excited about it, you might be correct and should pay attention to your feeling: If people are not energized by the idea or willing to commit to the group on a regular basis, they may, inadvertently, squelch the group's enthusiasm.

   Focus, therefore, on the people you believe are genuinely motivated and who, themselves, have a strong need for a supportive group. Keep in mind you only need a few people. Large groups don't function very well. Oftentimes, having only one other person (a pair, instead of a group) can be even more productive. Groups formed by three to five people are ideal, because when one or two members can't make it to a particular meeting, the others will be there to give and receive some feedback.

4. Once you've identified the group (or at least one other person), schedule and plan your first meeting. Spend a few minutes setting up an agenda for that meeting. At the first meeting, the group needs to decide on a few ground rules: meeting times, location, alternative location, how the time will be used, how much time will be allotted to the various tasks during the meeting, etc. List all items requiring discussion at your first meeting. Here are a few you will want to address:

   a. How will the group go about giving/receiving feedback? I recommend dividing the available time by the number of pieces requiring reading. For instance, three people bring something to read, and the group meets for a 1-hour time slot. Allot each piece 20 minutes: 10 minutes (or less) for reading, 10 minutes for a round of feedback for each piece.

   b. Members who have something to be read should bring enough copies of their writing so each member has a copy. Because time will always seem short, you might consider establishing a rule: Only two or three pages (double-spaced) will be looked at during each session.

   c. Will members need to do any homework before they meet? I strongly discourage this practice, although some groups function better when members have a chance to read each other's work beforehand. The reason I don't care for the idea is this: Most people already have so much to do; if they perceive the writing group as added work, they will be reluctant to join. If they do join, they will skip meetings when they haven't had time to read. Because you want people to learn to appreciate receiving feedback, the more you can make the writing group a place where writing gets better instead of a place of increased workload, the more the members will take ownership and invest their energy in the group sessions!

   d. Who will lead the meetings, keep track of time, ensure everyone provides and receives feedback, and be responsible for communicating with the group?

5. Hold your first meeting. Make notes of the group's decisions, and plan for the next session.

6. During the remaining practice sessions, spend 5 minutes writing/reflecting on the group, how it might contribute to your work, and what could be improved.

7. After each meeting, make sure you incorporate the suggested changes into your writing project during regular writing sessions.

EXERCISE 20—SCHEDULE READING APPOINTMENTS

TIME NEEDED: Setup: 05 minutes each writing session this week; actual meetings: 30–60 minutes each.

MATERIALS NEEDED: A more-or-less complete draft of your writing project

This last recommendation isn't really an *exercise* but a behavior you should consistently practice as a writer: As often as possible, *schedule reading appointments* to obtain feedback on your writing.

Students sometimes ask me, "When you have a few minutes, would you mind taking a look at the introduction I wrote for this paper?" I hate to admit it, but when I hear such a request, I cringe: When will I have a few minutes when I can honestly say, "Oh, I guess I'll read that student's introduction, because I have nothing else more urgent, important, or better to do right now . . ." Yes, I'm being sarcastic. In reality, though, I rarely "have a few minutes." As with most academic writers, even the minutes I spend on my own writing I have to carve or chisel into my rock-solid schedule—they don't just spontaneously *happen*. So the brutally honest answer is usually, "No, I won't have a few minutes; not now, not ever."

Because I don't want to be rude, however, I answer a bit more politely and simply say: "I'll be happy to read this *if* you schedule a meeting with me so we can read it together. Better yet, if I have something for which I need feedback, I'll read yours, and you'll read mine. Is that okay?" I try to make it clear: If the student schedules a meeting with me, he/she is certain to obtain feedback in the near future. If he/she just sends me the manuscript hoping those mythical few minutes will emerge spontaneously in my schedule, he/she might wait a long time with no feedback at all.

Scheduling reading appointments is a practice I learned from Tara Gray (2005). She recommends scheduling appointments with the expert readers, the ones who are usually too busy to add your manuscript to their to-do list. Yet, surprisingly enough, if you schedule a meeting and offer to read something of theirs while they read your paper, they are usually quick to respond and quite eager to do it—I know I am!

And please keep in mind: Although reading appointments are best during the final stages of your writing, if you need feedback from one of your colleagues on a middle-range draft, this is a good way to both *receive* and *provide* feedback. Therefore, for your exercise this week, do the following:

1. Identify the expert readers from whom you wish to obtain feedback.

2. Schedule an appointment with each one. If they are extremely busy, schedule a very brief meeting, a 15- or 30-minute appointment. You can obtain excellent feedback on only a portion of your writing; later, you will be able to incorporate that feedback into the entire piece.

3. Keep your appointment.

4. During the appointment, ask the reader to read only a few pages from your piece. Ideally, you should time the meeting so half the time (for instance, 15 minutes) is spent reading and the other half is spent talking about the writing, or exchanging suggestions for improvement.

5. Afterward, always remember to send your reader a special thank-you note (especially if he/she is a renowned expert in your field). Also, remember to return the favor by offering your services as a reader.

6. During the remaining practice sessions, write your reflections about the process: whether you would do anything differently in the future, whether you would recommend the practice to others; who are the other people with whom you might schedule a reading appointment; when can you schedule another one, etc.

7. Make sure you incorporate into your writing project those suggested changes you find appropriate and useful. Do this during your regular writing sessions.

References

Elbow, P. (1998). *Writing with power: Techniques for mastering the writing process* (2nd ed.). New York: Oxford University Press.

Elbow, P., & Belanoff, P. (1995). *A community of writers: A workshop course in writing* (2nd ed.). New York: McGraw-Hill.

Glanz, K., Rimer, B. K., & Viswanath, K. (2008). *Health behavior and health education: Theory, research, and practice* (4th ed.). San Francisco: Jossey-Bass.

Gray, T. (2005). *Publish & flourish*. Springfield, IL: Teaching Academy, New Mexico State University.

Lamott, A. (1994). *Bird by bird: Some instructions on writing and life*. New York: Anchor Books.

Rickard, C. M., McGrail, M. R., Jones, R., O'Meara, P., Robinson, A., Burley, M., et al. (2009). Supporting academic publication: Evaluation of a writing course combined with writers' support group. *Nurse Education Today, 29,* 516–521.

Chapter Six

Edit and Proofread

Only the hand that erases can write the true thing.

Meister Eckhart (1260–1326)

Think About It . . .

As your writing takes shape, you will focus less on generating new ideas and more on perfecting those already generated, so this chapter contains eight exercises for editing and proofreading your own text. Since writing *is* rewriting, we spend much of our writing time polishing, pruning, sharpening, and double-checking the text we generate. It makes sense, then, to devote some time to becoming proficient in both editing and proofreading.

Were you surprised when you read, "writing *is* rewriting"? It's true; if you want to write well, you must accept that you will be spending considerable time rewriting, rewriting, and rewriting some more. One of my favorite fiction writers, Michael Crichton—author of *Jurassic Park,* among other books-turned-movies—is credited with saying, "Books aren't written—they're *rewritten.* Including your own. It is one of the hardest things to accept, especially after the seventh rewrite hasn't quite done it."

Before we start, it is important to keep in mind the different *types* of rewriting we'll be addressing in this chapter: One type results from careful editing, the other from proofreading. Editing and proofreading are very different tasks; we engage in them *after* generating a lot of words and, hopefully, after receiving *useful feedback.*

But how does editing differ from proofreading? It's rather simple.

Editing entails organizing ideas, connecting sentences, moving paragraphs, reverse outlining, as well as making sure the appropriate structures are in place and the text *flows.* When carried out systematically, editing should move from broad to narrow: from the larger text to the smaller units, the words—from the structure of the whole piece to the structure of individual paragraphs to the structure of single sentences to the structure of simple phrases (see Figure 6.1). It makes no sense to start changing individual sentences or phrases—the narrowest level—when you're not sure you will keep them in your final version. The exercises in this chapter will help you avoid such a mistake by having you practice editing at the broad, overall-text level first and moving toward the narrow, specific-words level later.

Proofreading, on the other hand, comprises checking for errors and correcting inconsistencies in formatting, spelling, grammar, and punctuation. Whereas editing involves creativity and often requires the author to generate additional text to fill in certain gaps, in the proofreading stage, you are done generating. You are checking the minute details of formatting, spelling, punctuation.

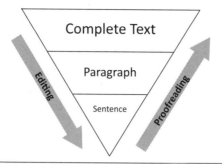

Figure 6.1   Editing and Proofreading as Separate Processes

Proofreaders are the professionals employed by newspapers and publishers to check whether the final proofs are ready to be printed. I would not want the job for all the money in the world! It's tedious, nearly impossible to do perfectly every time, and there's *always* a mistake in typing or setting that stubbornly slips through . . . ugh! My hat's off to those who help authors like me make their writing letter-perfect!

In the final exercise in this chapter, I will provide tips to practice proofreading your own work. While it's a true joy to find and clean up the little mistakes in your own manuscript, sometimes paying a proofreader is just easier or more practical. Personally, I prefer to proofread my own work before submitting it, just because I like to produce clean, final drafts. If you're too busy, however, and your time might be better spent generating the *next* piece, then, by all means, delegate the proofreading task to a competent professional.

Research Shows . . .

Kate Morss and Rowena Murray (2001) evaluated a program designed to facilitate writing strategies for various teaching and research staff at Queen Margaret University College in Scotland (the Writing for Publication, or WfP, project). The program comprised four group meetings over a 6-month period, alongside a "study-buddy" system, where faculty regularly met, in pairs, to "write, discuss progress, share strategies and to read and give feedback on text" (p. 39). A monitoring process that helped participants track their progress and monitor their goals was also part of the program. The evaluation sought to "track and monitor individuals on the programme in terms of their original goals from the outset, their interim goals and progress, their written output and their perceptions of the benefits in terms of outcomes" (p. 40).

After determining the program impacted all participants' writing productivity, the authors concluded:

> The experience of running the programme and the evaluation data suggest that confidence grows through a combination of a number of quite different activities: goal setting and deadlines, peer support, structured approach to writing, strategies for regular writing, strategies for making time for writing and protecting it. (p. 49)

EXERCISE 21—TIGHTEN THE PARAGRAPHS

TIME NEEDED: 15 minutes x session

MATERIALS NEEDED: Timer; your middle-range or semifinal drafts

When building an architectural structure, engineers need solid material. Most commonly, the material—whether bricks, stones, concrete slabs, or steel beams—comes in pieces, segments, blocks, or chunks. The engineers' task is to configure these chunks into a *structure*.

Structure refers to the placement of the parts within a system. A structure presupposes *organization:* an arrangement in which each part *relates to* or *connects with* the other parts, as well as with the whole. Within an academic text, structure refers to the organization of the *whole text* as well as to the relationships among its sections, paragraphs, and sentences.

A good structure relies on complete, strong, and stable building blocks. In academic writing, it helps to think of *paragraphs* as your text's building blocks. Paragraphs—more-or-less complete thought units—function as the chunks of raw material you need to mortar and bind as you engineer your structure.

In all writing genres, but particularly in academic writing, paragraphs have a structure (or an organization) of their own. The paragraph's structure in academic writing seems awfully boring for creative writers, but it works well for communicating ideas among scholars and other professionals concerned with a bottom-line take-home message.

A "tight" academic paragraph's internal structure consists of the following parts:

(TRANSITION) + ONE KEY IDEA + DEVELOPMENT OF KEY IDEA

Take note, because this is the only place in the entire book where I offer you a tested-and-tried *formula* (we're all searching for formulas to simplify our work, aren't we?). If you follow this formula, you will have tightly knit paragraphs and your text—as a whole—will move quickly, maintain its focus, and communicate clearly.

Here's an example of a tight paragraph:

A paragraph should also be consistent in structure; that is, it should complete three functions in order. First, the paragraph should open with a transition. The transition can be as short as a word or a phrase that was used in the previous paragraph—or as long as a sentence or even two or three. . . . Second, the transition should be followed by a topic or key sentence. Third, the rest of the paragraph should provide support or evidence for the idea in the key sentence. As you revise, you should check each paragraph against this template. (Gray, 2005, p. 42)

What makes this paragraph solid? Read it again. Identify which sentence holds the main idea. Highlight it. Then, examine everything else in the paragraph. If a transition is not linking this paragraph to what came before, it should directly connect to the key idea. (Note: Connections are made by providing definitions, examples, data, or comments about the key idea, *without introducing any new concepts*. Keep in mind, you may also connect ideas simply by repeating words.)

Take a second look at the example:

KEY IDEA: a paragraph "should complete three functions in order."

TRANSITION: "A paragraph should **also** be consistent in structure" (you don't have the text that came before, but Gray was discussing how paragraphs should be consistent in their *length*).

ALL OTHER IDEAS/SENTENCES: The sentences beginning with *first, second,* and *third* clarify the key idea—"three functions in order"—presented in the first sentence.

NOTICE: No other salient concepts or ideas are introduced in this paragraph. There are no tangents or detours into other ideas that are new to the reader.

In contrast to the example above, here's a paragraph I've made up, which introduces a second key concept and, therefore, loses its structure:

A paragraph should also be consistent in structure; that is, it should complete three functions in order. First, the paragraph should open with a transition. Transitions are essential for connecting the current paragraph to the previous one(s), and without transitions authors may lose their readers as the paragraphs begin to read like bulleted lists of ideas. Bulleted lists might be very useful in certain parts of the text, but they aren't fully developed text. Many readers don't appreciate bulleted lists.

Can you see how this example represents a poorly structured and loosely coupled paragraph? What affects its structure and makes it "loose"? The ideas *do seem to flow*, don't they? The reason they appear to flow is because each sentence connects to the previous one. Yet, the *paragraph lacks structure* because not all sentences are *tied to the original key idea.*

KEY IDEA: A paragraph "should complete three functions in order."

TRANSITION: "A paragraph should **also** be consistent in structure."

SENTENCE #2: "First, the paragraph should open with a transition." This sentence *does* tie directly to the key idea because it develops the notion of functions a bit more.

SENTENCE #3: "Transitions are essential for connecting the current paragraph to the previous one(s), and without transitions authors may lose their readers as the paragraphs begin to read like bulleted lists of ideas." As I begin to talk about transitions (the idea in Sentence #2), notice how I drift away from the key idea in the paragraph (the idea of completing three functions). I've also begun to introduce slightly new concepts I didn't develop previously: losing readers, readers not liking to read bulleted lists of ideas.

SENTENCE #4: "Bulleted lists might be very useful in certain parts of the text, but they aren't fully developed text." Again, notice how far I've moved away from the *key idea* in the paragraph (that of a paragraph's structure completing three functions). Now, I'm having my reader focus on something very different from what I proposed to talk about in the beginning of the paragraph.

SENTENCE #5: "Many readers don't appreciate bulleted lists." When you ask yourself, "Does Sentence #5 develop, clarify, or provide an example/evidence for the key idea in the paragraph (the idea of completing three functions)?" you will notice how far removed from the main idea this sentence really is!

If I insisted on keeping that loosely connected paragraph in my text and then attempted—in the next one—to talk about the second and third functions, the reader would become confused, frustrated, and lost.

One of the best things you can do for your writing, therefore, is to put into practice this week's exercise: Every time you have written enough text, check the building blocks—or paragraphs—you are engineering.

1. Set your timer for 15 minutes.

2. Begin with the first paragraph in your text.

3. Ask yourself: Which sentence in this paragraph contains the key idea?

4. Highlight the sentence in a bright color.

5. If you're writing on a computer, cut and paste the highlighted sentence into a new file.

6. Label the new file "Key Sentences" (we will come back to this file in Exercise 22).

7. Of all other sentences in the paragraph, ask: Is this a transition? If not, does it connect to the key idea/sentence directly? Do not skip any sentence in the paragraph.

8. When you find sentences that do NOT connect, you have a choice: Either

   a. pull them out (i.e., break the paragraph), or

   b. reword them so they *do connect* to the key idea.

9. Continue checking, one by one, every paragraph in your text in this manner.

Caution! This exercise can become very tiresome and boring; therefore, you'll be tempted not to do it. However, because this is a highly useful strategy for improving the quality of your writing, I recommend you arm yourself with patience and tackle the chore in small chunks: Do only 15 minutes today, 15 minutes tomorrow, and so on. The exercise will feel less like a drudge. As you begin to see the benefits, you'll become more motivated to practice the strategy, and to implement it routinely.

Among all the excellent tips or techniques I have learned, if I had to choose the best strategy to check my writing for flow, this one would be my top choice. Therefore, I strongly recommend you make this exercise a routine practice—not merely a sporadic one—incorporating it from now on into everything you write or edit.

EXERCISE 22—MAKE IT FLOW: ORGANIZE

TIME NEEDED: 15 minutes x session

MATERIALS NEEDED: Timer; the Key Sentences file you developed in Exercise 21

Most of us learned we need to make an outline in order to begin writing. Here's my take on this: *DON'T*. Don't outline to begin writing. Unless you know *exactly* what you want to say, in the *precise order* you want to say it, don't use an outline to generate text. I'll argue, instead, you should outline *from the already generated text* to verify that it is well organized.

Daphne Gray-Grant (2008), in *8 1/2 Steps to Writing Faster, Better,* also encourages writers to "resist outlining" when they are beginning a writing project. She has a convincing argument: She claims outlining is a *terrible* idea. Alright . . . this portion of her argument may not be very convincing. But the rest might persuade you: Outlining requires analytical, logical, or formal thinking. Analytical is the type of thinking most appropriate for editing or revising and least appropriate when generating new ideas or creating new text. During the generating phase, outlining can lead to writer's block, because when you are thinking creatively, your thoughts are not neatly organized; they're scattered, messy, and incomplete. That's the nature of newly generated text, at least for most writers. Forcing the generating into tightly outlined categories stifles creativity and leads to blank-stare-at-the-screen syndrome. On the other hand, for editing text after you've generated enough, for checking whether your text has the appropriate sections, and ensuring sections connect with each other in an orderly manner, outlining can be a very useful tool!

Generating outlines in this manner is known as *reverse outlining* (Belcher, 2009). This week's exercise focuses on developing a reverse outline and using it to check the organization of your text, how smoothly it flows. Here's what you need to do:

1. Set your timer for 15 minutes.

2. Open the Key Sentences file you developed during the previous exercise. (If you haven't worked on Exercise 21 yet, practice that one first; you will then have the Key Sentences file you'll need for this exercise.) If you're working from a paper printout, use the draft where you highlighted the key sentences in a bright color. This file (or your color-highlighted sentences), for the moment, constitutes your outline. The question is, "Does this outline reveal a *structure?*"

3. Read the key sentences out loud slowly. This is easier if you have generated a file with key sentences only. The purpose is to focus solely on them, not on the surrounding text.

4. As you read, ask yourself: Are the key ideas presented in an *orderly manner?* Do I present the ideas in a *chronological or logical order?* Does this list *look* like an outline, as though I had begun my writing with one? Does a structure emerge? Do the pieces fit together harmoniously?

5. While reading slowly, you'll begin to identify the gaps, the holes between key ideas where you skipped from one concept to the next without providing the necessary information for your reader to follow. Perhaps you will notice, too, that the idea in Key Sentence #10 should be the first paragraph in your text. Gaps and disorganized ideas will pop out at you in ways they never did before, even though you've just read your entire text over and over again, trying to check for flow.

6. Make notes on the Key Sentences file about any further text you need to generate to fill in the gaps.

7. If needed, play with moving your sentences around: Place Sentence #10 at the top of the file. Recheck the sequence among the sentences that follow: Does the new arrangement improve the flow?

8. Go through the Key Sentences file slowly, 15 minutes at a time. This exercise also may be tiring, but resist the temptation to skip it. Stay with it; do a little bit at a time.

9. I recommend you do ***not*** make changes to your full text until you have gone through the entire Key Sentences file. If you make a change immediately after catching a problem, you may become confused, losing track of which changes you made and which ones you left for later. Trust me on this one: It is worthwhile to delay editing the text until you've carefully read and examined *all* key sentences.

10. Once you've completed reading the key sentences and determined which changes you will make, return to your full-text file and tackle each change, one at a time. As you move ideas around, don't forget you're moving entire paragraphs: This may affect how the paragraphs connect. Therefore, after completing the necessary paragraph moves, read your text out loud once again, paying special attention to transitions and connections between each paragraph and the next.

This exercise—especially if you can paste the key sentences into a separate file—will allow you to see key ideas *out of context.* As you examine them in a new light, undressed from their paragraphs, you will have fewer distractions and be better able to gauge how well the *key ideas connect,* whether the text flows.

Example

Here's a snippet of a Key Sentences file I created when I was writing my book on theory in health promotion. I have numbered the sentences for easier reference.

Chapter 8—Key Sentences

Guidelines for applying theory to research

1. We completed our journey through the current theoretical landscape in health promotion.

2. Realistically, I hope the journey also prepared you to accept the fact that this theoretical landscape is what it is, and you and I have to deal with it, despite its imperfections.

3. To respond to these questions I would like to offer you some guidelines.

4. I would like to propose the guidelines I will offer you in this chapter are *not* rules set in stone, procedures to be followed in a lockstep fashion.

5. Once you've developed and established your own pathways, discard these guidelines.

6. Please note each set of guidelines I propose in this chapter (and in the next) can be found in an abbreviated, checklist format at the end of the chapters, so you can actually check off each of the steps as you complete them.

7. You may choose not to read the entire chapter but focus on the sections that seem more relevant to *your* project.

As I reread just these key sentences (mind you, I'm reading these at least 2 years after the book was published), I still can see an order, a logical sequence to the ideas. Do you see it? I stumbled, however, in one spot: Sentence #3. Its key idea doesn't connect well with what came before, because I wasn't talking about questions the readers might have. Hum . . . this is a problem. The outline breaks down here. I have to make a decision.

Looking back, I can't recall my thought processes at that moment, but I would venture to say they may have gone something like this: Perhaps if I *added* another key idea, between Key Sentences #2 and #3, mentioning the questions, then the flow would be perfect as I move from the topic of questions to the topic of guidelines. I would, then, make a note on my draft saying, "Add paragraph here," and point to the space between Sentences #2 and #3, like this:

2. Realistically, I hope the journey also prepared you to accept the fact that this theoretical landscape is what it is, and you and I have to deal with it, despite its imperfections.

Add
paragraph
here

3. To respond to these questions I would like to offer you some guidelines.

Notice that the ideas in Sentences #6 and #7 don't connect well either. In #6, I'm talking about a checklist at the end of the chapter; in #7, I mention this notion of sections, which I have not presented previously, in the key sentence. Again, I need to decide whether to reword something in the paragraph containing Sentence #7, discard it, or add another key idea between Sentences #6 and #7 (remember: every time you add a key idea, you're adding a paragraph).

EXERCISE 23—CLEAR O~~UT~~ THE CLUTTER

TIME NEEDED: 15 minutes x session

MATERIALS NEEDED: Timer; the semifinal drafts you now have, after checking each paragraph for its key sentence

Editing your work involves going through your text, line by line, catching and doing away with all the "stylistic faults that most often impede reading and obscure meaning" (Cook, 1985, p. viii). As writers we get so close to our texts, we are unable to catch many of the most glaring problems even though we read and reread our work. What we lack are a few strategies we can apply in a systematic manner, strategies that—regardless of how close we are to the text—will still raise the red flags in our writing.

If you search, you will find countless books and online resources to help you edit your own work. If you're desperate for time, however, or would rather have surgery than tackle the tedious job of editing your writing sentence by sentence, you'll also find myriad editors advertising their services for a fee. These books, websites, and editors can be invaluable resources, especially during busy or difficult times.

Even so, I would argue the best investment you can make in the *quality* of your writing is to take on the hard, meticulous task of editing yourself. Why? Because editing your own work is an investment that continues to yield dividends on your writing-skills capital. Learn to edit and correct your work; practice it once, twice, 300 times: You'll begin to see your initially shitty drafts become better and better, cleaner and clearer. Editing your own work improves the *quality* of all your writing. No other investment pays higher or better dividends.

Among the many resources available to help you edit, the most famous one is also the shortest: Strunk and White's (2008) *The Elements of Style*—a small book that celebrated its 50th anniversary edition in 2008. The book is about the need for clarity and brevity in written text. Above all, the authors argue for "cleanliness"—for decluttering text of anything that renders it *clunky, confusing,* or *messy.* A quick glance at the topics covered in Chapter II provides a sense of what Strunk and White aimed for:

II. ELEMENTARY PRINCIPLES OF COMPOSITION (Table of Contents)
   12. Choose a suitable design and hold to it.
   13. Make the paragraph the unit of composition.
   14. Use the active voice.
   15. Put statements in positive form.

16. Use definite, specific, concrete language.
17. Omit needless words.
18. Avoid a succession of loose sentences.
19. Express coordinate ideas in similar form.
20. Keep related words together.
21. In summaries, keep to one tense.
22. Place the emphatic words of a sentence at the end. (p. viii)

As you can see, decluttering involves several different steps, and sometimes deciding where to start is difficult. The exercise for this week attempts to simplify the process a bit by offering a simple *checklist system* for tackling these steps. The checklist adapts Strunk and White's recommendations together with those made by other authors such as Richard Lanham (1999), Claire Kehrwald Cook (1985), and Tara Gray (2005).

1. Set your timer for 15 minutes.

2. Refer to the checklist presented below.

3. Search your entire text for *only one* element from the checklist at a time. For example, start by doing an edit/find in your word processor or by highlighting in your hard copy each time the preposition *of* appears.

4. After highlighting all occurrences, study each highlight: Is this particular *of* introducing a clunky or wordy phrase? Could the phrase be shortened? Could you eliminate the preposition altogether? For example, say the first *of* in your text appears in a sentence such as this:

   The epidemic of childhood obesity has become a problem of significant proportion worldwide.

   By highlighting the two *of* forms, you quickly notice you can eliminate the first one by rewording the noun phrase like so: "the childhood obesity epidemic." In the second instance, *of* appears in a wordy phrase. You can shorten it considerably to "has become a significant problem worldwide."

5. Correct or make changes to your text only after you've highlighted all instances of the word you're checking (see the checklist below for other words for which you will search). If you identify and correct, simultaneously, you risk not being systematic in your checking and missing many problems along the way.

6. Repeat exactly what you did for *of* with each word in the checklist. Check off each round on your list. If you limit yourself to only 15 minutes per session, it will take several sessions to finish, yet the time you spend will serve two invaluable purposes: (1) It will clean, tighten, and make your text flow more quickly, smoothly, and clearly; and (2) you will come up with a better way to say things. Over time, this effort will begin to show in your drafts, and your final edits will become easier!

Checklist for Decluttering Your Text[1]

Search for the elements listed below, in successive rounds:

- ☐ Of
- ☐ That/which
- ☐ This/that/these/those
- ☐ Verb *to be* (in all forms): is/was/will be
- ☐ Words ending in *-tion* and *-ment*
- ☐ And/as well as/too/or
- ☐ Useless words
- ☐ Subject-verb agreement

In the summary matrix presented in Table 6.1, you will see how searching for each element on this checklist can improve your text. The matrix describes the types of problems most frequently found in each search round and provides examples.

Tip for ESL Writers

For even more opportunities to practice decluttering and improving your writing, overall, I recommend using one of the resources listed below. During each writing session, read one to two pages from the book you choose and practice one recommendation each session.

1. *Style: Ten Lessons in Clarity and Grace*, by Joseph M. Williams (2010)

2. *The Elements of Style*, by William Strunk, Jr. and E. B. White (2008)

3. *Line by Line: How to Edit Your Own Writing*, by Claire Kehrwald Cook (1985)

4. *Revising Business Prose*, by Richard Lanham (1999)

Reading these texts in small portions and practicing the strategies outlined by the authors will yield both a faster-moving text and cleaner drafts. You will slowly internalize these strategies and write less-messy drafts the next time!

Table 6.1   Types of Problems One Can Diagnose Through Consecutive Editing Rounds

When you search for . . .	You may find . . .	Examples
Of	Wordy prepositional phrases. These can be shortened or eliminated. Without them, your text moves faster, reads easier, and becomes less cluttered.	*I took the course of which students had spoken.* *Better: I took the course students recommended.*
That/which	In writing, we can eliminate *that* 90% of the time. Checking for *that* and *which* also will identify wordy sentences, as well as faulty word placement. In this case, we need to remember what Cook (1985) cleverly stated in *Line by Line* regarding the geography of words: **"When words aren't near the words they go with, they go with the words they're near"** (p. 18).	We might say, *I need to tell her that she's looking great today!* When we write (instead of talk), we can omit the *that* with no loss whatsoever: *I need to tell her she's looking great today!* Example: *The sentence we talked about in the first exercise that we gave as an example is too wordy.* In this example, by highlighting *that* we notice its placement makes the meaning of the sentence ambiguous: Are we saying "the exercise we gave as an example" or "the sentence we gave as an example"? Better: *The sentence we discussed in the first example is too wordy.*
This/that/these/those	Potential ambiguity. Here, again, we're reminded of Cook's (1985) mantra: **"When words aren't near the words they go with, they go with the words they're near"** (p. 18).	Example: I was tempted to use the word *this* to begin the last sentence you read in the left column. I wanted to write: *For clarity, avoid using this and that. Repeat the concept or the idea to which the words refer. **This** will ensure clarity and avoid potential ambiguity.*

(Continued)

Table 6.1 (Continued)

When you search for . . .	You may find . . .	Examples
	Look for sentences **beginning** with *this*, *that*, *these*, and *those*. Ask yourself: What does *this* refer to? Remember, for the reader, the word *this* refers to what is geographically close to it, usually the last word(s) or concepts before the period in the previous sentence. For clarity, avoid using *this* and *that*. Repeat the concept or the idea to which the words refer. Repeating will ensure clarity and avoid potential ambiguity.	As soon as I wrote it, I noticed I was using *this* to refer to *repeat* in the previous sentence. The geography is problematic, however: There is considerable distance between the words *repeat* and *this*, so the reader becomes confused whether *this* refers to *idea* (the concept closest to *this*) or to *repeat*. I decided, therefore, to change my sentence: *Repeating will ensure clarity and avoid potential ambiguity.* Here's the whole thing, rewritten: *For clarity, avoid using this and that. Repeat the concept or the idea to which the words refer. Repeating will ensure clarity and avoid potential ambiguity.*
Verb to be **(in all forms):** **is/was/will be**	Passive voice. In passive voice, the subject of the sentence passively *receives* or *suffers* the action expressed by the verb, rendering the action weaker. Active voice, on the other hand, has the subject actively carrying out the action. Active voice makes sentences more dynamic; they move quicker. Making subjects passive tends to weaken the sentence, making it "less direct, less bold, and less concise" (or more wordy)—say Strunk and White (2008). Because passive forms are constructed with the verb *to be*, finding the verb will help you catch and change your uses of passive voice.	Example: *The decision was made by the president of the organization.* In the example above, the action is *making a decision.* Verb: *decide.* Who is deciding? *The president of the organization.* Better: *The president of the organization made the decision,* OR *The president of the organization decided.* Plus, if you're searching for *of,* you can eliminate the one in the sentence above quite easily: *The organization's president decided.*

When you search for . . .	You may find . . .	Examples
	Of course, at times, you *want* to keep the passive form because you wish to place emphasis on the subject, not on the action. When that is the case, keep the passive voice. However, avoid overusing it because it makes reading difficult and/or boring. To solve the problem, do this: Decide what the action is. Ask yourself "What is being done?" Name the action with an active verb (Gray, 2005; Lanham, 1999). Decide who is doing it. Identify the subject or the agent in that action. Turn the sentence into a subject → verb → object sequence.	
Words ending in -tion and -ment	"Ponderous nouns"—a term used by Cook (1985, p. 6) in *Line by Line*. Words ending in -tion and -ment—used abundantly in academic writing because they sound scholarly—produce writing that is wordy, "lifeless and noun-burdened," making the reading both "dull and difficult" (p. 6). Examine each instance in your writing where you use these ponderous nouns. Ask yourself whether you do, in fact, need them or if a shorter, clearer term might make the writing communicate better.	Example: *During the evaluation of the reading program, frustration and disappointment were detected among program personnel, whereas during the program's development, such feelings were unimaginable.* Better: *When evaluating the reading program, evaluators met staff who felt frustrated and disappointed. When staff were developing the program, however, these feelings were hard to imagine.*

(Continued)

Table 6.1 (Continued)

When you search for . . .	You may find . . .	Examples
And/as well as/too/or	Faulty parallel forms, wordy sentences, and "unbalanced pairs" (Cook, 1985). According to Cook, You can detect most errors in parallel structure by routinely checking the words or word groups you join by *and* and *or* and making sure that they match. In other words, the elements linked as compound subjects, objects, verbs, and modifiers should have the same grammatical form. When they don't you can either bring them into line or change the structure to eliminate the need for parallelism. (p. 55)	Example: (taken from the draft of a grant proposal I wrote): *Anomalies. That is how persons who have tested positive for HIV infection, **and** have refused to submit to mainstream treatments, **and** live for a decade or longer without developing AIDS are viewed by mainstream science **and** health care.* When highlighting all the *ands* in the segment above, I notice the sentence's structure is not parallel: *have tested, have refused, live.* Better: *Anomalies. That is how persons who have tested positive for HIV infection, have refused to submit to mainstream treatments, **and** **have survived** for a decade or longer without developing AIDS are viewed by mainstream science and health care.* Even better (if I eliminate the passive voice "are viewed by mainstream science" and use *yet* instead of *and*): *Anomalies. That is how mainstream science and health care view persons who have tested positive for HIV infection, have refused to submit to mainstream treatments, yet have survived for a decade or longer without developing AIDS.*

112

When you search for . . .	You may find . . .	Examples
Useless words	Deleting these words makes your text sharper, tighter, and clearer without losing any intended meaning.	Example: *In this study I will examine interviewees' narratives of their real-life experiences.* Consider eliminating *real*. If it is their life experiences you're examining, they should be *real* (at least for the person you are interviewing). Consider eliminating *real life*. The experiences can only be theirs, if it happened during their lifetime. So, why not just say, *In this study, I will examine interviewees' narratives of their experiences.* If you still want the notion *of life* in that sentence, how about using *lived*, like this: *In this study, I will examine interviewees' narratives of lived experiences.*
Subject-verb agreement	Grammar mistakes you can easily correct. This involves checking each sentence in your paper, one-by-one, and focusing on one sentence at a time. You may find it easier to edit if you examine your sentences out of context. The easiest way to do this is **to read each section in your manuscript** *backward.* Begin with the Discussion section, for instance. Read and check the last sentence in that section, then check the next-to-last sentence, then the one before, successively.	Example: *Primary care providers and the public health workforce **enjoys** the privilege of working on the prevention side of health care.* The sentence has two subjects, *providers* and *workforce*; so the verb should be *enjoy*, not *enjoys*. When we're writing it is easy to focus exclusively on the last word we wrote (*workforce*) and automatically make the verb agree with it (*workforce enjoys*). It's only in the editing stage that we catch these slips (ideally, you would have caught this one when reading out loud [see Exercise 27], but you may not have, especially if you were doing the reading yourself).

EXERCISE 24—USE A THESAURUS AND A REVERSE DICTIONARY

TIME NEEDED: 20 minutes the first session; 10 minutes each session thereafter

MATERIALS NEEDED: Timer; portions of your text that require editing

This exercise introduces ESL writers to a thesaurus, because I have learned that many of my international students are not familiar with this tool. Native English speakers may think the exercise is not useful to them because they already use a thesaurus when they write. Yet, here, I also discuss using a reverse dictionary, a resource many ESL and English speakers know nothing about and may find helpful. Together, these tools are indispensable for writing well and for decreasing the stress associated with editing our own writing. They help us consider different words for the same concept so we can safely avoid monotonous repetitions and write with precision.

Writers of every nationality know about dictionaries—the compendium of words and their definitions, which is widely available and easy to access (especially now, with online dictionaries). Dictionaries are invaluable, but while they help us write with *precision,* they don't necessarily help us write *with elegance.*

A thesaurus, on the other hand, helps polish our writing. Why? Because it provides equivalent terms, or synonyms, for a specific word or phrase. Some thesauri also provide antonyms. Having a list of words with the same (or very similar) meaning helps avoid nonelegant and unnecessary repetitions. For a brief presentation on thesauri, see the "Tip for ESL Writers" in Chapter 3.

A reverse dictionary also is a must-have tool, especially for ESL writers. Have you ever written a sentence in which you needed a one-word description for, say, an action? If I were writing a sentence about John and Jane, and what I really wanted to say was that John complimented Jane on a recent award she received, it might take me 14 words to describe precisely what I meant (something like, "John couldn't stop complimenting Jane and commenting on how much she deserved the award and how happy he was she had won it!").

Using a reverse dictionary, however, I can search for a one-word term describing much of this. When I search for "pay a compliment," for instance, I find these verbs as potential substitutes for my long explanation: *praise, applaud, greet, salute, honor.* I choose the word *applaud,* so my sentence becomes: "John applauded Jane's recent award."

A thesaurus and a reverse dictionary are tools you should routinely have next to you while writing. When I'm editing my own work, I always have an online thesaurus open on my computer, and I consult it several times during the process. But let me emphasize one important point: Use these tools only when you're *editing* your work. Don't waste time consulting them while generating new thoughts. When generating, it doesn't matter: Repeat the same word three times; use 12 words to say what you can—later—say with a single verb. Remember, you should use generating time to produce lots of words, regardless of their appropriateness. Using a thesaurus or reverse dictionary while generating text is counterproductive. Only when you're in the editing phase do these resources become effective.

This week's exercise, then, is this:

1. Find a thesaurus you can use—purchase one if you'd rather have a bound copy. There are numerous options in the market. I love my pocket-size *Oxford Desk Dictionary and Thesaurus* (1997). For some reason, despite all the "cool" tools now available on the Internet, I often refer to this well-worn paperback. Other options I frequently use are these (you may find others you like better):

   www.visualthesaurus.com—This site charges a reasonable annual fee. Once you pay the fee, you have access to many writing-related tools and newsletters, including a word-a-day e-mail, which we discussed in Exercise 9. The site also allows you occasional free access, if you're checking just a single word. In this case, you will be limited to the trial version.

   www.onelook.com—This site has a useful dictionary function, which searches a given word in multiple dictionaries, simultaneously. What I find most helpful, however, is the reverse dictionary. You find it by going to OneLook and clicking on the "Reverse Dictionary" link (at the top of the page). Reverse dictionary gives you a one-word equivalent to a long phrase. OneLook describes it this way: "OneLook's reverse dictionary lets you describe a concept and get back a list of words and phrases related to that concept. Your description can be a few words, a sentence, a question, or even just a single word."

   http://poets.notredame.ac.jp/Roget/—*Roget's Thesaurus of English Words and Phrases* gets my vote for absolute favorite resource! It provides synonyms of a term, organized by that term's dimensions of meaning. For instance, if you search the word *academic,* it returns the synonyms organized into three dimensions: supposition, teaching, and school. Depending on how you're using the term, you choose which meaning you intended and the thesaurus will display all the nouns, verbs, adjectives, and adverbs related to the term, under that dimension of meaning. Some of these words would never occur to you as related to *teaching* or *academic,* but they might become appropriate substitutes in your writing. For instance, you may not associate the word *book* with the term *academic,* if you were writing a sentence such as, "He has considerable academic knowledge." Yet if you were writing this sentence and you had already used the term *academic* three or four times, you might substitute the phrase *book knowledge:* "He has considerable book knowledge."

2. Once you've identified a tool you may want to use, plan to spend 10 minutes during each writing session this week playing with it and becoming familiar with its features. You'll also need to have a piece of your own writing to edit. It need not be a long piece, just enough so you can practice.

3. During each 10-minute practice session this week, attempt to find better, more precise, and even—as many of you are quite frequently trying to do— more academic terms to substitute for the ones you wrote in your text.

4. Caution! Avoid terms unfamiliar to most readers. If you do use an unfamiliar term, always make it a point to define it, unless you've made the meaning very clear from the context.

Example

If I wanted to edit the paragraph I just wrote above using a thesaurus and a reverse dictionary, I could come up with something like this:

BEFORE: Caution! Avoid terms unfamiliar to most readers. If you do use an unfamiliar term, always make it a point to define it, unless you've made the meaning very clear from the context.

AFTER: Note, however: Avoid employing strange or unfamiliar phraseology. If you utilize such phrases, consider always defining them, unless you are rendering them easy to understand based on their circumjacent context.

To some of you, the edited text comes across as much more formal and academic (and, therefore, better) than the unedited text. But notice how stuffy it sounds, and how—for others of you—it borders on artificial because most people don't talk like that. Despite your preference, at least you've become acquainted with options and resources to improve your text.

But remember to use care: Making your text sound academic may, in fact, obfuscate (complicate, conceal) the clarity of your message. Do not sacrifice clarity for an academic-sounding writing style. When you do, you're writing in jargon. According to William Zinsser (1988), jargon is "the lingo of people in specialized fields who have infected each other with their private terminology and don't think there's any other way to say what they mean" (p. 66). He cautions:

More often jargon consists of special terms that every occupation has found it necessary to invent. Used with restraint, they aren't jargon: they are the working tools of a particular field, and if they serve a specific need we have no trouble learning new ones overnight: words like "amniocentesis" and "gentrification" and "superconductivity." The trouble arises when jargon becomes a crutch—when its users become so dependent on their private terminology that they claim they can't express themselves in any other way. Social scientists, for instance, are addicted almost beyond mortal help. Consider these two sentences from a book by a famous sociologist. I didn't choose them as exceptions; the whole book is in this style.

"The third major component of modeling phenomena involves the utilization of symbolic representations of modeled patterns in the form of imaginal and verbal contents to guide overt performances. It is assumed that reinstatement of representational schemes provides a basis for self-instructions on how component responses must be combined and sequenced to produce new patterns of behavior." (pp. 67–68)

I would bet one month's salary on this: Even sociologists reading these sentences would have to reread at least three times in order to understand them! Please, *please,* have mercy on your readers, even on those who share your professional jargon!

EXERCISE 25—PAY ATTENTION TO WORD PLACEMENT

TIME NEEDED: 10 minutes x session

MATERIALS NEEDED: Timer; portions of your text that require editing

In Strunk and White's (2008) famous book, the authors make the following recommendation:

> The position of the words in a sentence is the principal means of showing their relationship. Confusion and ambiguity result when words are badly placed. The writer must, therefore, bring together the words and groups of words that are related in thought and keep apart those that are not so related. (p. 28)

Their explanation is another way of saying:

When words aren't near

the words they go with,

they go with

the words they're near.

I know: You have already read the quote above (from Cook, 1985, p. 18) at least three times in this chapter. I hope you have memorized it by now. It will come in handy during your editing.

Yet this particular issue concerning word placement—how position within the space of a sentence influences meaning—is not the only word placement dimension we need to consider. Another aspect we should pay close attention to is *placement for emphasis: Where* a particular word or phrase appears in a sentence highlights, emphasizes, or spotlights that word or phrase. Conversely, certain places in a sentence bury a word, make it less important, less visible, even less meaningful. Here's an example:

POOR PLACEMENT FOR EMPHASIS:

The global pandemic of human immunodeficiency virus (HIV) infection is now well over two decades old. Much has been learned from it, and many ongoing challenges have presented themselves during this time.

BETTER PLACEMENT FOR EMPHASIS:

> The global pandemic of human immunodeficiency virus (HIV) infection is now well over two decades old. Much has been learned from it, but its duration provides continued as well as new challenges. (Whitaker, Vogele, McSherry, & Goldstein, 2006, p. 311)

Notice how the first words in Sentence #1 present the global pandemic, and the last words in Sentence #2 introduce the idea of challenges. In the poor-placement example, the challenges idea hides within the compound sentence and loses its emphasis. By placing the word *challenges* at the very end of the sentence, the authors highlight their main point, with little effort.

As we polish our writing, then, we need to concern ourselves with these two aspects of word placement: (a) potential ambiguity and (b) emphasis. Below, I describe two exercises, each focusing on a specific aspect.

To catch problems belonging to the first dimension of word placement— potential ambiguity—practice this exercise:

EXERCISE A—Word Placement and Ambiguous Meanings

1. Set your timer for 10 minutes.

2. Sentence by sentence, look for all the nouns in your text and highlight them.

3. Examine the words close to that noun. Are the modifiers near the noun? Or are they *waaaaaay* over there in another part of the sentence?

4. Move words around to fix your word placement problem, as needed.

5. After you've tackled all the nouns in your text, do one round for the verbs (checking for misplaced adverbs).

Here's an example of problematic writing, involving misplaced complements or verb modifiers. This piece was allegedly sent to the (now defunct) U.S. Welfare Department by a citizen trying to claim certain benefits:

> I want my money as quickly as I can get it. I have been in bed with the doctor for two weeks and he doesn't do me any good. If things don't improve, I will have to send for another doctor.

If you search for verbs in Sentence #2, you will highlight *have been.*

In bed modifies *have been*, very well. But *with the doctor* does not go too well with *in bed* (unless the writer really meant to say he/she is sleeping with the doctor). *For two weeks* qualifies *have been in bed*, so it should move closer to that portion of the sentence to read:

I have been in bed for two weeks.

Further editing could move *the doctor* closer to *doesn't do me any good* to read:

I have been in bed for two weeks. The doctor hasn't done me any good. If things don't improve, I will have to send for another doctor.

While the exercise above helps you recognize problems due to potentially ambiguous meanings, the next exercise will help catch issues belonging to the second dimension of word placement: emphasis.

EXERCISE B—Word Placement and Emphasis

1. Set your timer for 10 minutes.

2. Examine your text, sentence by sentence. (To break the monotony, choose paragraphs randomly or begin with the last paragraph in the text and work backward.)

3. Ask yourself: Where did I place the key idea in this sentence? If needed, play with moving words around until you get the emphasis or vigor you desire.

4. Work this way, sentence by sentence, through your entire manuscript.

5. Note: This is another one of those tiring exercises, especially if you don't like to edit. For this reason, do it in small chunks over several days. As you notice how much you can improve your text, you will get hooked on doing this kind of polishing. Better yet, you will become so tuned in to proper word placement, even the rough drafts you write in the future will be much, much better!

Tip for ESL Writers

Because writers whose first language is not English sometimes have difficulty using articles, or the words *a*, *an*, and *the*, I recommend these tips I found in Bruce and Rafoth's (2009) *ESL Writers: A Guide for Writing Center Tutors*.

1. Perform one round of editing for all the noun phrases in the text. "Noun phrases consist of a noun and any modifiers it may have" (p. 106).

2. See if you can use the word *one* in front of your noun phrases. If you can, it may be that you need to use *a* or *an*.

3. If using the word *one* works, but you don't want just *any one*, you want a *specific one*, then use *the*.

These steps will not work all the time, but coupled with having your text read out loud (by a native speaker, if possible), they will serve as a useful editing strategy. This strategy will help you learn how to use the articles without having to recall grammar rules each time you write. Give it a try!

EXERCISE 26—CUT IT IN HALF

TIME NEEDED: 10 minutes x session

MATERIALS NEEDED: Timer; semifinal drafts of your work

Once in a while I face the problem of producing too long a text and needing to cut down. Some writers think this is a nice problem to have, because they find generating a lot of words a difficult task. But I am a wordy writer who wants to explain everything and make my points crystal clear. Yet I will often overlook how this can be done—*without* compromising any of the intended meaning—using fewer words. In fact, as William Zinsser (1988) reminds me, "Most pieces can be cut by 50 percent without losing any substance" (p. 65).

Even if you are not required to cut down your text to a specific word limit, I still highly recommend this exercise, just to eliminate the clutter your text may have accumulated during the generating stages. And in those cases where you are required to cut down your text, the exercise works like a charm!

1. Set your timer for 10 minutes. Focusing on small chunks of time over several writing sessions will make the task less tedious. You also will be able to pay closer attention to it.

2. Go over your text and delete ONE WORD from every sentence.

3. When you're done deleting one word from every sentence, it's time for the second round: Delete ONE SENTENCE from every paragraph.

4. When you finish that round, go for the third round: Delete ONE PARAGRAPH from every section.

5. Finally, in the last round, delete ONE SECTION (yes, a whole section, if you can!) from the entire piece.

6. After doing this, if you still have not achieved the required word count, start again: one word, one sentence, one paragraph. You will soon have edited your piece down to a much more manageable size. Likely, you also will notice that nothing essential is missing from your report. Nothing you cut out was really needed for your account to make sense and to flow smoothly. In fact, sans excess clutter, you are probably communicating much more clearly and efficiently.

7. In summary, you will be doing multiple rounds to DELETE

   a. from every sentence, ONE WORD;

b. from every paragraph, ONE SENTENCE;

c. from every section, ONE PARAGRAPH;

d. from the entire piece, ONE SECTION

. . . until you reach the required word count or the polish you desire.

EXERCISE 27—READ ALOUD

TIME NEEDED: 10–15 minutes x session

MATERIALS NEEDED: Timer; your middle-range or semifinal drafts

Reading your own work aloud is a frequent recommendation made by professional writers of all genres (especially by fiction authors). Peter Elbow, the great theoretician of the writing process, not only advocates for reading out loud, he also explains *why* it is valuable. In a draft chapter from his new book, Elbow (2010) poses the question, "How does reading aloud improve prose [writing]?"

> A satisfactory answer turns out to be complex and interesting, but I'll begin with the simple claim that I use with first year students: Readers will find your writing clearer and more inviting when your language is comfortable to speak aloud. When it is, readers don't have to work as hard to understand your words. They seem to *hear* the meaning come up off the page. (p. 5)

Specifically, Elbow (2010) suggests reading aloud can help you detect problems such as "roundabout or long winded language," "bureaucratic prose," "repetition," and "interruptions" (pp. 10–11). All these elements will scream out at you as your text is being read aloud. They will catch your attention, for sure.

This exercise will take between 10 and 15 minutes of your practice sessions this week, or, if you prefer, you may choose to devote one longer session to reading your entire text.

1. Set your timer for 10 or 15 minutes.

2. Print a hard copy of your semifinal draft, if you're working on a computer file. Yes, print (or recycle, if you don't like to waste paper). It's important to change the look of your text. Just by changing the medium (from computer screen to paper), you are able to recognize important mistakes throughout the text.

3. Read your text aloud, *s-l-o-w-l-y.* Pretend you are approaching this text for the first time.

4. If you are fortunate enough to have a writing partner, schedule this exercise for a meeting time and ask your partner to read the text out loud to you. It is easier to catch problems with our writing when we hear it being read in

someone else's voice. Your reader will also help you catch instances of poor wording, run-on sentences, and awkward usage.

5. If you do not have a writing partner who can read for you and you've grown so accustomed to the text you don't see the problems any longer— even when you read it out loud yourself—I suggest having your computer read it for you. You can configure a computer to read your text out loud; just look in the set-up menu for the features designed to assist users who have visual disabilities. Alternatively, some software packages such as Adobe Acrobat can read text for you (after you convert your file into a PDF format). Having the computer read your text has both advantages and disadvantages. The advantages are you don't have to find someone else to read it, and you still get to hear your text read out loud by another voice. The disadvantage is the computer has no intonation and reads without any nuance, in a flat, mechanical voice (much like the computer voices used in old sci-fi movies). Even so, just having your text read in a different voice will make some problems pop out. As a side note, I had Adobe Acrobat read this whole chapter for me when I was editing because I had lost my voice after conducting several workshops and couldn't read it out loud myself. I was surprised at how many problems the mechanical voice allowed me to catch!

6. During the reading, you have two options: rework each problem as you catch it, or just mark the place that needs attention and proceed reading the entire text.

7. Repeat this reading-out-loud exercise more than once with semifinal and final drafts. Make it a routine practice not to submit any writing for review without at least one round of careful, out-loud reading.

EXERCISE 28—COPYEDIT: PROOFREAD LINE BY LINE

TIME NEEDED: 20 minutes the first session; 10 minutes x session thereafter

MATERIALS NEEDED: Timer; semifinal drafts

By the time you finish writing and editing, you will have read through the text many, many times. It's not uncommon to do 20-plus rounds of editing, in some cases. You become so acquainted with the words you wrote, you no longer notice the small mistakes. Typos, extra spaces, inconsistencies in font type, paragraphs that are indented versus separated by line spacing . . . it's all a big blur.

This exercise will help you catch these problems through one or two additional rounds of proofreading.

1. When you first do the exercise, set your timer for 20 minutes. For all other sessions, set it for just 10 minutes.

2. During the first session, I recommend you spend the 20 minutes developing a style sheet for your piece. Editors usually recommend creating a style sheet at the beginning of a project (Sullivan & Eggleston, 2006). I don't develop mine right at the beginning but prefer to build it as I write the text.

3. A style sheet is a file (or just a sheet of paper, if you're not working with a computer) containing all the decisions you make related to how your piece should look. Decisions such as the font type used in your headings, whether first-level headings will be bolded, whether second-level headings will be in italics, whether you will indent the first line in each paragraph or separate paragraphs with an extra line space, and so on. This sheet also should contain the decisions regarding issues of consistency. For example, the first time you mention the National Institutes of Health, you write the full name, then follow it with the acronym (NIH) in parentheses. After that, all references to the Institutes will use the acronym only. Finally, the sheet should contain your decisions regarding spelling and capitalizing. For instance, throughout the manuscript, will you write *health educators* or *Health Educators?*

   Consistency in all these details is important, no matter which format you choose. Ignoring details signals sloppy work to reviewers, and a well-written paper will not be perceived as well written if it comes speckled with these apparently minor inconsistencies. By developing a style sheet and capturing all these decisions in one place, you don't have to rethink every time you encounter the term *National Institutes of Health* in your paper and decide: Should I leave it spelled out, or should I use the abbreviation? Your style sheet will tell you what to do. In the generating phase, you can write without worrying about being consistent, confident you will be able to catch all the problems later in the proofreading stage.

It is important to note that we often must follow a particular style when we write (such as American Psychological Association, Modern Language Association, American Medical Association, among others), either because the publishers want the text formatted in a specific way or because our field has committed to writing in a certain style. In such cases, your style sheet has already been developed for you. All you have to do is use the reference manual for that particular style.

Yet I find these style manuals daunting and the details I need often difficult to find quickly. Therefore, even when using a required style manual, I still recommend developing your own personal style sheet *and* developing a new one for each writing project. They are much easier to refer to than an entire style manual when you're proofreading, and your style sheet will contain all your manuscript's idiosyncrasies.

Here's a typical example of what I would place in a style sheet:

Paragraph formatting: Indent first line; no space after paragraphs

Heading Level 1: ALL CAPS, bold font, Times New Roman (TNR) size 12

Heading Level 2: First Letter Capitalized, bold font, TNR size 10

Text: Normal, TNR size 10

Usage: health educators—not capitalized

4. Once your style sheet is ready, return to your final draft.

5. Reformat your final draft: Make it look completely different from what you have had in front of you so far. Change the font type, font size, format the text into two columns—change everything. By doing this, you will see your manuscript differently. The little mistakes you couldn't catch because you had seen them so many times will now pop out.

   When I'm writing a journal article, I like to reformat my text to simulate the final product. So, using a word processor, I will *select all* the text, single-space and column-format it. I will also change the font type to one more like what the publisher uses. I make the title big, bold, trying to emulate those in the journal where I'm submitting.

   You don't have to change very much: Just changing the font type and enlarging it will make small, buried problems leap from the text.

6. After reformatting, print a hard copy of your text. At this stage, switching from computer screen to paper really helps in catching mistakes. If you are not working on a computer, merely copying your text on different-colored paper will help change its look and give you a new perspective.

7. With the reformatted, hard copy of the text and your style sheet in hand, begin editing the text, line by line. I recommend editing once from start to

finish, then once more from finish to start (backward). As you read along, mark the problems but don't correct them until later, after you've captured them all.

8. It's important to s-l-o-w d-o-w-n during these final rounds. If you're having difficulty slowing down, here's a tip I often use: Highlight the line you are editing with a colored marker, then switch highlighters when it's time to examine the next line. Notice I said *line*, not sentence. During this process, you are no longer concerned with meaning, only with form, with how the words look on paper. So focus on one line of text at a time. Proceed, alternating highlighter color for each line. Mark all the mistakes. This switching back and forth really forces you to slow down and pay close attention.

   If using the markers slows you down too much and you just can't stand it (!), try using a ruler or a blank sheet of paper to hide all the remaining text, isolating the one line you're working on. This will slow you down but not as much as changing highlighters will.

9. After you've finished marking the entire text, return to the beginning to correct each mistake.

10. If necessary, do one more round of problem searching. This time, begin with the last line in the text and move backward, line by line.

Example

Here's an example of how changing the look of your text allows you to capture problems more easily. Here's the text in normal draft view:

> The statistics on the Administration on Aging website (an office of the Department of Health & Human Services) reveal that, in the United states the number of people aged 60 -65 years is expected to double between the years 2006 and 2030 (from 12.4% of the U.S. population, to 20 percent of the U.S. population. See http://www.aoa.gov/AoARoot/Aging_Statistics/index.aspx

Now, here's the reformatted text before editing:

The statistics on the Administration on Aging website (an office of the Department of Health & Human Services) reveal that, in the United states the number of people aged 60 -65 years is expected to double between the years 2006 and 2030 (from 12.4% of the U.S. population, to 20 percent of the U.S. population. See http://www.aoa.gov/AoARoot/Aging_Statistics/index.aspx

In the reformatted text, it's much easier to spot, among other errors, that the first line in the paragraph is not indented; that I used the % sign and also wrote the word *percent;* and that I failed to close the parenthesis after the citation. Did you notice any typos as you read the original format? Note also the period after *population,* before the citation; it should follow the closing parenthesis. Here is the corrected paragraph:

The statistics on the Administration on Aging website (an office of the Department of Health & Human Services) reveal that, in the United States, the number of people aged 60–65 years is expected to double between the years 2006 and 2030 (from 12.4% of the U.S. population to 20% of the U.S. population—http://www.aoa.gov/AoARoot/Aging_Statistics/index.aspx).

Note

1. This checklist borrows from suggestions made by various authors, including William Strunk, Jr. and E. B. White, Claire Kehrwald Cook, Tara Gray, and Richard Lanham.

Electronic Sources

Elbow, P. (2010, January). Revising by reading aloud: What the mouth and ear know [draft chapter from forthcoming book]. Retrieved from http://works.bepress.com/peter_elbow/33/

OneLook Dictionary Search: www.onelook.com

Roget's Thesaurus of English Words and Phrases: http://poets.notredame.ac.jp/Roget/

Visual Thesaurus: www.visualthesaurus.com

References

Belcher, W. L. (2009). *Writing your journal article in 12 weeks: A guide to academic publishing success.* Thousand Oaks, CA: Sage.

Bruce, S., & Rafoth, B. (Eds.). (2009). *ESL writers: A guide for writing center tutors* (2nd ed.). Portsmouth, NH: Boynton/Cook.

Cook, C. K. (1985). *Line by line: How to edit your own writing.* Boston: Houghton Mifflin.

Gray, T. (2005). *Publish & flourish*. Springfield, IL: Teaching Academy, New Mexico State University.

Gray-Grant, D. (2008). *8 1/2 steps to writing faster, better*. Vancouver, BC: Highbury Street Books.

Lanham, R. (1999). *Revising business prose* (4th ed.). New York: Longman.

Morss, K., & Murray, R. (2001). Researching academic writing within a structured programme: Insights and outcomes. *Studies in Higher Education, 26*(1), 35–52.

Oxford desk dictionary and thesaurus (American ed.). (1997). New York: Berkley Books; Oxford University Press.

Strunk, W., & White, E. B. (2008). *The elements of style* (50th anniversary ed.). New York: Longman.

Sullivan, K. D., & Eggleston, M. (2006). *The McGraw desk reference for editors, writers, and proofreaders*. New York: McGraw-Hill.

Whitaker, R., Vogele, C., McSherry, K., & Goldstein, E. (2006). The experience of long-term diagnosis with human immunodeficiency virus: A stimulus to clinical eupraxia and person-centered medicine. *Chronic Illness, 2*, 311–320.

Williams, J. M. (2010). *Style: Ten lessons in clarity and grace* (8th ed.). New York: Pearson/Longman.

Zinsser, W. (1988). *Writing to learn: How to write—and think—clearly about any subject at all*. New York: Harper & Row.

Part II

Practice Writing Sections of Journal Articles, Research Reports, and Grant Applications

Chapter Seven

Exercises for Writing Introductions, Purpose Statements, or Specific Aims Sections

Summary

Think About It . . .

EXERCISE 29—Map

EXERCISE 30—Dump

EXERCISE 31—Craft the Purpose Statement

EXERCISE 32—Develop the Rationale

EXERCISE 33—Present the Literature Review

EXERCISE 34—Lay Out the Theoretical Framework

EXERCISE 35—Check It

Checklist for Introductions

*Put the argument into a concrete shape, into an image, some
hard phrase, round and solid as a ball, which they [the readers]
can see and handle and carry home with them, and the cause is
half won.*

Ralph Waldo Emerson (1803–1882)

Think About It . . .

Writing introductions to journal articles or book chapters, along with
purpose statements or specific aims sections in grant proposals,[1] usually
scares academic writers as much as brain surgery. Patients can count on
anesthesia to get them through brain surgery; authors writing introductions
aren't quite so lucky. The reason for the apprehension lies in the inherent
difficulty of writing these sections. The difficulty, in turn, stems from the
multiple expectations embodied in an introduction: It must engage the
reader quickly; it must clearly lay out the road map for the reader's journey; it must state the purpose unambiguously; it must provide enough historical background on the topic. Composing text to achieve *all* these goals
simultaneously, while adhering to strict page or word limits, may seem like
a mammoth task—and, well . . . I hate to say it, but it is! It's a lot to ask
of a writer! Those who are less experienced often balk at the challenge or
desperately wish there was such a thing as writing anesthesia, preferably in
pill form.

Fear of tackling introductions is why most scholars recommend that you
begin with the methods section, leaving the introduction for last. I don't
recommend this strategy, unless you are so completely paralyzed by fear,
you're not writing anything. Better to be working on the methods section
than not working at all. Yet beginning your piece by rough-drafting the
introduction has several advantages, which I explore below.

Before we examine these advantages, however, a quick side note: To
ease communication throughout this segment, I'm going to assume you are
writing either journal articles for peer-reviewed journals in the social and
behavioral sciences or grant proposals for federal funding agencies. Even
though most recommendations and exercises are equally applicable to other
forms of academic writing, such as term papers, book chapters, reports, or
books, I will employ language referring to articles and grants.

If you begin drafting your piece with the introduction, you will have the
chance to capture your current thoughts and to note their changes over
time. It's important to start the capturing process *early* so your ideas can

mature. Begin, then, by writing down all your thoughts for the introduction without worrying whether the ideas are good or bad, coherent or incoherent, accurate or inaccurate. As your writing progresses, many ideas placed in the intro section will later be moved to the discussion or methods, but it is important to capture them *somewhere, right now.* At this point, however, don't worry about producing a final, polished introduction. Simply begin capturing the ideas of how to "enter" into your topic.

Another advantage you gain by starting with your introduction is this: You will have a better idea of what to present or discuss in the other sections. In the introduction you'll need to frame your piece. In other words, you'll need to tell your reader what to expect—what is your purpose and what you will argue for. This framework will become a personal blueprint for writing the methods, results, and discussion. In those sections you will write *only* about the elements that fulfill the purpose you stated in the introduction,

Research Shows . . .

In 2002, Linda J. Sax and her colleagues published a study examining research productivity among a sample of 8,544 full-time teaching faculty from 57 universities in the United States. The data were part of the 1998–1999 Higher Education Research Institute Faculty Survey. The authors assessed the role of "marriage, children, and aging parents" as potential influences on productivity after controlling for other factors.

Among their findings were these:

a. While the gender gap in productivity appears to be closing, it "remains unchanged among highly productive faculty (those producing five or more publications within a 2-year period)" (p. 428): In research universities, 31.1% of men had five or more publications within the 2-year data period, compared with 20.0% of women.

b. Bivariate statistical analysis (uncontrolled) showed "being married or with a partner is associated with higher publication rates for men" (p. 430).

c. In statistically controlled analyses (controlling for rank, salary, research orientation), family-related variables made only a tiny contribution, "suggesting that once key demographic, institutional, and professional variables have been controlled, family-related factors have little influence on faculty research productivity" (p. 430).

the elements that fit your framework, and you will have a much clearer idea of *what* to write.

If you retrofit the introduction to what you presented in your paper (i.e., if you write the introduction *after* drafting the methods and results), you may find it hard to connect all the elements described in your presentation. Some elements may not connect with others easily, may take the reader on tangents, or may be difficult to combine into a single, coherent point. It's much easier to bake a cake if you use a recipe that calls for certain ingredients and only those. It's much harder to scatter various ingredients on your kitchen counter, then ask yourself, "Now, let's see . . . can I make a cake using some of these?" You may, in fact, succeed, but you also run a huge risk of failing! Better to start with a recipe to guide the baking. Better to have at least a draft of an introduction to set parameters for the remainder of the paper.

In this chapter I will not go into much detail on *how* to write or organize an introduction or specific aims section. To learn *how*, you can refer to many available resources (some of which I've listed in the Appendix). I provide, instead, several exercises to help you *practice* writing introductions and purpose statements/specific aims. To help you a bit with *how* to write an introduction, I have posted a journal-article writing template on the book's website (at www.sagepub.com/goodson), which you can use more or less as a fill-in-the-blank form. The template will remind you to include certain elements from your research you may not have thought about writing. It is merely a tool to help you think; it's *not intended* to be an exhaustive, comprehensive, all-encompassing model. I do realize that for some fields of study the template is not appropriate because those fields' research reports follow a different structure. Even if you belong to an area of study that does not use written reports formatted in this structure, the template may help you consider a few things you should always include in any introduction section. It serves as a useful checklist, if nothing else. Take a look!

EXERCISE 29—MAP

TIME NEEDED: 15 minutes x session

MATERIALS NEEDED: Timer; blank sheets of paper and colored pens/pencils, or mind-mapping software

In this exercise you will practice mind mapping. Mind mapping has become a popular tool since Tony Buzan developed it in the 1970s (About ThinkBuzan, 2011). It helps you think out loud and draw your thoughts. Mapping generates a graph, a one-page, at-a-glance picture of the many connections your mind makes while thinking about a topic.

If you are the kind of author who likes to outline, you will probably enjoy using a mind map, too. Listing ideas in a linear format—one word or phrase after the other—as we do when we outline, doesn't provide an at-a-glance big picture of your text. A mind map, on the other hand, keeps the whole image in sight—showing all the dimensions and connections among them, along with their details.

Mind mapping is a fabulous instrument for generating new writing ideas, for structuring various writing pieces, as well as for capturing all the associations one makes while thinking through a writing project. Mind mapping has, in fact, become a widely used tool for many academic-related tasks such as improving students' retention of learned material; facilitating creativity; teaching or learning different concepts; planning and organizing; presenting ideas, projects, and reports; and solving problems in teams (see "Why Mind Mapping Works," 2011). It is especially useful for writing introductions, or for thinking through the structure of an entire paper or grant proposal.

You can draw a mind map using simple tools: paper (usually a blank sheet, in landscape position, so you have more room to draw) and pens, pencils, or colored pens and markers. You can also rely on available software packages designed to perform more complex tasks, such as attaching a PDF file to the ideas in your map or sharing electronic maps among members in a writing team. If you search the Internet for available software packages and strategies for developing mind maps, you will unearth a range of applications and information—from the most simple to the most sophisticated. (Please note: I could not do justice to the topic if I attempted to teach you in this book how to mind map. I recommend, therefore, that you find tools to learn about the process on your own. The resource list in the Appendix offers a few citations and places on the Internet you can check out to start.)

This week's exercise, then, consists of mind mapping your introduction.

1. Spend one practice session learning how to draw a mind map (even if you use only pencil and paper—the way I develop most of my own mind maps). It will take just a few minutes to learn. Use the first practice session exclusively for learning how to use the tool. I've included two examples of mind maps in this chapter (Figures 7.1 and 7.2). Studying these examples, you will have an idea of how to draw your own mind maps.

2. In the next practice session, mind map your introduction or specific aims section. (Note: You also may find mind mapping useful, later, for brainstorming each section in your paper or proposal. You may also try developing a mind map for the entire paper so you can keep the big picture in mind while you work on each individual section.)

3. Don't worry about completing the mind map during the first session. The idea is to allow the map to mature, over a few days, before actually writing the text. Keep adding to your map during each practice session this week.

4. As you're building your mind map, there will come a point when you sense you have enough to begin writing. When you reach that point, start developing the text using your mind map as a guide. But remember: Your map is never set in stone or definitive. As you write, you may find yourself making new associations, thinking about other aspects of the text you hadn't thought about previously. Capture those aspects in writing, and, later, add them to your mind map if you want to keep the maps as documents of your thought process.

Example

Below are two examples of mind maps I created. The messy-looking, hand-drawn mind map (Figure 7.1) reflects my initial thinking about a paper I wished to write regarding health education faculty's roles and expectations when working at universities with high research emphasis (formerly known as Research 1 institutions). The second, neater-looking map (Figure 7.2) represents a first attempt to capture my thinking related to a health education ethics course I was developing. The map is not even close to being complete or exhaustive; it merely captures my initial thoughts about how the course *might* be structured. The course's final format contained many of the elements in this graph, but some never made it into the last version (for instance, I omitted the "brief history of health education" module).

As you can see in these examples, there isn't a single right format for drawing mind maps, yet the principle remains the same for each: Capture as a snapshot all the dimensions of a given topic in their dynamic relationships. I always stand in awe of how mind maps—due to their snapshot quality— allow me easily to recall both the big picture and the details of a project I'm working on, even when I step away from it for some time. Give it a try!

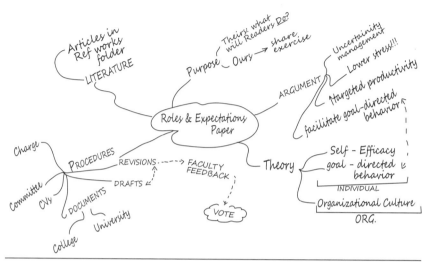

Figure 7.1   Example of Hand-Drawn Mind Map

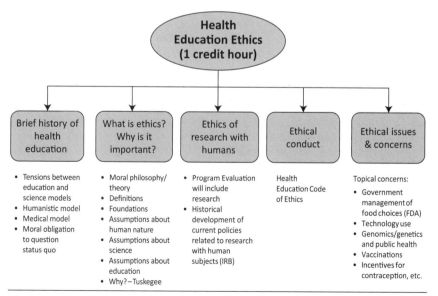

Figure 7.2   Example of Mind Map Drawn in PowerPoint

EXERCISE 30—DUMP

TIME NEEDED: 15 minutes x session

MATERIALS NEEDED: Timer; your mind map

For this exercise, do the following in each practice session during the week:

1. Open a clean word processor file (or get a blank sheet of paper) and write "Introduction" or "Specific Aims" at the top. List several useful subheadings—you may have developed these in your mind map last week—representing the various pieces or segments in your introduction.

2. Use these subheadings as you would use the drawers in a file cabinet. Start by dumping words into these drawers. Yes, dump: as if you had a box full of junk and you were going to pour it all into those drawers for later sorting. Dump all the words and ideas twirling around in your mind: the well-formed, mature ones; the potentially good, embryonic ones; as well as those for which you have no clue whether they might be good or bad, useful or trashcan-worthy. Dump potential connections you might make and even the questions you have about your yet-to-be-written article. Using your timer, dump for 15 minutes nonstop. The only rule here is this: Do not stop to think. Write as fast as you can everything that comes to mind about the article, including any thoughts about the findings and results. Write in your native language if you don't recall the proper words in English. Just make sure you address everything you originally placed in your mind map—everything you still find relevant, that is. Don't bother about correct spelling, punctuation, or even complete thoughts. Write notes to yourself as you dump, question yourself, talk to yourself as you go (see the example).

   As you dump, you dive into your paper, and, over time, as your brain feeds on the ideas you're capturing, it massages and shapes the information for you. A common practice of mine is to begin these dumping sessions by writing, "*I have no clue how I want to structure this article or which perspective I want to emphasize here.*" I may even write thoughts similar to these several days in a row, until, all of a sudden, there's a moment when I know exactly how to proceed (it surely *seems* as though it's all of a sudden, but it results from sitting down with the topic several times).

3. Don't forget, the introduction is the place in your report where you want to talk about

   - the PURPOSE of the manuscript/grant (WHAT?),
   - the RATIONALE for what you propose to do (WHY?),
   - the BACKGROUND for your purpose (WHEN? WHO?), and
   - the THEORETICAL support for your purpose (HOW?).

4. Close your file after the practice session ends.

5. When you return to practice, organize your mess, moving ideas that more properly belong in other drawers, throwing out apparently useless ideas, adding bits and pieces you're just now remembering.

    Caution! Never throw away any writing when you're still drafting a piece. Create a TRASH file inside the folder containing your project and copy and paste into that file everything that, at this moment, you consider garbage. If you're writing by hand, label a hanging or manila folder "Trash" and file the page with the discarded ideas in this folder. Later on in your project you may need to use some of those trashed ideas.

6. Spend each writing session this week focusing on the introduction: dumping and organizing, dumping and cleaning. Eventually, you'll be spending less time dumping and more time editing. You will see your introduction begin to mature, the ideas begin to take shape, and the desired direction for your text begin to materialize. Give it a try!

Example

Here's an example from my own writing. I copied and pasted this introduction, verbatim, from my writing journal. Notice the spelling and punctuation mistakes, the rough transitions and lack of continuity, as well as the notes to myself as I tried to capture what was on my mind about the article:

This study reports on findings from a state-wide evaluation of abstinence-only-until-marriage programs implemented in the state of Texas between XXX and XXX (years). Programs evaluated in this study received Title V funding for their programs. Title V funding entails (explain what Title V is—maybe look at the book I'm reviewing for JSR—they may have a nice, concise explanation, so I don't repeat what I've said in previous papers about Title V. Need also to explain what AUM programming is, and what it's main purpose/ focus is all about. Perhaps mention that programs aim at changing ytouth's perceived norms about abstinence being "cool" given that one of our findings was related to dosage and perceptions of peers (the uncontrolled finding).

> **Tip for ESL Writers**
>
> Use mind mapping to diagram the introduction of other authors' articles that you judge to be well written. To do this, map all the headings and subheadings you find in that introduction and its main points/arguments. This list becomes the skeleton of that article's introduction. Compare various skeletons of introductions. This will give you ideas for generating the structure for your own.

EXERCISE 31—CRAFT THE PURPOSE STATEMENT

TIME NEEDED: 10 minutes x session

MATERIALS NEEDED: Timer; the drafts you generated last week for introduction or specific aims sections

While you dumped and organized your introduction last week, you may have started to draft a purpose statement of sorts. This week, you'll spend time zooming in on that purpose or the specific aims portion of your text.

A clearly written purpose statement is the soul of a paper or proposal; it is the point toward which everything converges in the writing. If well written, the purpose statement becomes the climax of your introduction drama: the vertex, the focal point in your entire report.

Have you ever noticed how well-written novels keep readers on the edge of their seats? The purpose statement in your manuscripts represents your chance to create such a cliffhanger moment, to bring your readers to the edge of their seats and leave them there, balancing for dear life, while you carefully unveil the answers to all the intractable mysteries in the remainder of your report. Okay . . . I exaggerated a bit, but some of the best academic writing I have read manages to do precisely that: present the purpose of the piece in such a way, I can't help myself; I *have to read* the paper to learn more about it!

This exercise will allow you to spend some time practicing writing your purpose statement. With practice, you will be able to write those powerful, cliffhanger statements that make your reader *beg* to read the remainder of your text.

1. In the first practice session (10 minutes), write as many variations as you can of the answer to this question: *What is the purpose of this paper/report/ proposal?* Remember that, most often, the purpose is to *do* something: *answer* a question, *test* a hypothesis, *compare* findings across studies, *argue* for a better solution, *examine* a problem in depth, or *analyze* data in a new way.

   As much as possible, keep your purpose statements ACTIVE. In other words, always use verbs to describe your purpose, not nouns.

Example

DO write something like this:

The purpose of this paper is to *argue* for an alternative approach to *analyzing* data on adolescent sexual activity. We *present* four arguments supporting Jones's (2005) proposal to analyze such data from a dynamic systems perspective, instead of applying an individual-level approach.

DO NOT write something like this:

A proposal to analyze adolescent sexual activity data from a dynamic systems perspective is offered by Jones (2005). Jones's proposal is against applying individual-level analyses to these data. In this paper we are in agreement with Jones's position and rationale.

Notice that in the second example it is never quite clear *what* the authors will *do* in the text. None of the verbs are *action* verbs, so the reader remains uncertain of what will be presented.

As a side note: I have a colleague who reviews for several professional journals in sociology. He once told me he will refuse to review a manuscript if he cannot quickly find the sentence *"The purpose of this paper is . . ."* in its introduction. Although I do not refuse to review based on this criterion, when I review my students' papers or articles for a journal, I also look for that purpose statement, hoping to find it rather quickly either in the very beginning or at the end of the introduction section. If the statement or an equivalent is missing, I have an important clue: The manuscript might have significant problems related to clarity and organization.

2. As you brainstorm various ways to word your purpose statement, consider writing the purpose as a question, not as a statement.

INSTEAD OF . . .

The purpose of this paper is to argue for an alternative approach to *analyzing* data on adolescent sexual activity. We present four arguments supporting Jones's (2005) proposal to analyze such data from a dynamic systems perspective, instead of applying an individual-level approach.

TRY SOMETHING LIKE . . .

Would analyzing data on adolescent sexual activity from a dynamic systems approach provide an advantage over an individual-level analysis? Because we believe (with Jones, 2005) there is merit to this alternative, we present four distinct arguments supporting a dynamic systems perspective for analyzing data on adolescent sexual activity.

Did you notice I began the example above with a question? Have you also noticed that most good fiction writing (the type of writing we *enjoy* reading) centers on questions? Roy Peter Clark (2006) reiterates this point in *Writing Tools: 50 Essential Strategies for Every Writer*:

> Who done it? Guilty or not guilty? Who will win the race? Which man will she marry? Will the hero escape or die trying? Will the body be found? Good questions drive good stories. (p. 150)

And good questions can drive good academic writing as well. If you want to hook readers and make them *want* to read your paper, use questions. I even recommend using a pointed question to begin an article: First sentence. Right there. For example,

INSTEAD OF BEGINNING AN INTRODUCTION WITH THIS:

> Childhood obesity has become an epidemic in recent years; many scholars would argue that the epidemic has spread worldwide.

TRY BEGINNING WITH THIS:

> Has childhood obesity become a *pandemic* in recent years?

There's nothing wrong with the first example; it's just boring and repeats information most readers who are professionals in health promotion or nutrition already know. An opening sentence such as that one does *not* make me really interested in what else you might have to say, even if it ends up being intriguing (Casagrande, 2010).

By offering your readers a question, you immediately engage their thinking about the issue even if they are already familiar with the topic. A question invites readers to think and engage in a conversation with you. You've brought them to the edge of the cliff: They will not want to put your article down until the question is answered. You've hooked them into reading your paper.

3. At this stage, do not worry about editing your purpose statements; just write them in as many different ways as you can. End your practice session after the 10 minutes are up. Return to these statements tomorrow. Then, if necessary, dump some more. You'll think of other ways to craft the statement during the day, for sure!

4. During your subsequent practice sessions, tweak your previous statements, and add, edit, and play with them. Generate more, if you're still not satisfied with what you've done so far. But keep generating/editing in small chunks of time.

By allowing yourself to spend 10 minutes each session working on your purpose statement or specific aims, after six sessions you will have devoted at least 1 whole hour to working exclusively with the soul of your paper or proposal. And as the statement matures, you will also gain clarity on how best to frame the introduction, which aspects to emphasize, which lens to use. Keep referring back to your original mind map. At some point, however, you will see the text you've begun to write come alive: It will grow around that original mind-map skeleton and become stronger and richer. Eventually, you will no longer need your mind map.

After a week's practice, you should have a rather decent final purpose statement for your manuscript or proposal. Write the statement in large, bold letters. Print it. Post it on your writing station (next to your computer screen or on a wall; keep it in sight at all times). The purpose statement represents your most important guidepost, the most relevant road map for what you will write next. Everything you write, from now on, must be tightly linked to that purpose statement. *Everything.*

Tip for ESL Writers

Choose several articles in your field that your colleagues consider well written. If you're writing a grant proposal, ask for good models from the funding agency (if available) or see if some of your successful colleagues are willing to share their funded proposals with you.

Examine closely how the purpose statements are worded in these pieces, how the specific aims sections of the proposals are crafted. Notice the details: What kinds of verbs did the authors use? What details did they present? Did they do anything special or different to make the reading a bit more engaging or interesting? As you examine these models, take notes and try to do similar things with your statements. Try several different versions; vary your statements. Then, choose the best one for the final product.

EXERCISE 32—DEVELOP THE RATIONALE

TIME NEEDED: 15 minutes x session

MATERIALS NEEDED: Timer; your purpose statement (or specific aims section)

Whereas the purpose statement declares WHAT you'll be doing or presenting in your article, report, or proposal, the rationale explains WHY you chose to do it or present it. Far too often writers think about rationales as the portion of the introduction where they will explain why the topic is important and why it merits examination and discussion. And this is usually the extent to which researchers develop their rationale.

Yet when the author provides more than one rationale in a piece of writing, that piece becomes stronger. *"More than one?"*—you might ask. What other reasons should be provided, aside from the ones explaining why the topic is important? What else is there to explain *why?*

Describing the reasons why the author chose a certain *approach* or *methodology*—in addition to explaining why the topic is worth studying—strengthens the manuscript by a quantum leap. And if you really want to raise the quality of your work, provide a rationale for the statistical (or data analysis) strategies you've chosen to apply to the data. Note: The rationale for the *statistical* (or *data analysis*) strategies can be provided in the methods section; you don't have to include it in the introduction. Nevertheless, you can practice writing all your rationale segments as you write the introduction and later move the rationale for the statistical analysis to the methods section.

1. Based on the previous drafts you've developed thus far, identify the various rationales you want to present. Label and list these segments in your text. For instance, let's say you determine you want to write a rationale for

   a. the problem/issue/topic of the manuscript,
   b. the methodological approach or study design you chose to use (e.g., qualitative inquiry rather than a survey design), and
   c. the data analysis strategies you employed in your study.

2. Use the dumping-and-cleaning strategy you practiced a couple of weeks ago: Write down all the reasons for the choices you made (the choice of topic, approach, analysis). If appropriate, make notes to yourself to find adequate citations to support your choices. Grounding your rationale in authoritative citations will give readers more confidence in your decision. They will learn you chose qualitative inquiry over a survey design, for instance, not because they suspect you hate statistics but because you concluded that a qualitative

approach is the best choice, the best way to *know* your subject matter. In dumping, you may find it helpful to complete the following sentences:

a. The topic I chose to study is important *because* . . .
b. The approach I'm taking in this study is unique, or is the best one for my purposes, *because* . . .
c. The strategies (or statistical techniques) I chose for analysis are the best ones for my data *because* . . .

Make it a point to use the word *because* several times in your text. *Because* functions as a marker for the readers. When they see the word, they are primed for a rationale, a reason, an explanation. High-quality manuscripts (as well as reports and grant proposals) use the word *because* repeatedly.

3. After dumping, end your practice session. Return to what you wrote tomorrow.

4. Tomorrow, clean, edit, and reorganize your reasons. Add other reasons if you've thought of more since you stepped away from your writing.

5. If you choose, move the rationale for your analyses to the methods section (open a new file for the methods section if you don't have one already). Keep only the rationale for the topic, for your theoretical perspective, or for your overall approach in the introduction section.

6. Spend time this week cleaning, adding, and reorganizing a bit every day. Allow the reasons you've presented to mature over a few days. Don't forget to check your space or word limits and to keep the rationale segments short (in most cases, one or two sentences will suffice).

Example

Examples of rationales supporting the choice of a given research topic abound in the literature. Less common are instances of rationales supporting methodological choices. Below are examples of the latter.

The first example comes from the dissertation written by one of my doctoral students (now an assistant professor). She offers a rationale for the research paradigm she chose, backed by an authoritative source:

Qualitative research methods are unsurpassed for researching problems/phenomena for which the variables are unknown and need to be explored (Creswell, 2005). (Garcia, 2011, p. 36)

Another example explains the choice of statistical analysis. In this paper, coauthored by another former doctoral student and me, we wanted to make clear why we had chosen to use Structural Equation Modeling (SEM) to examine sexual abstinence among adolescents:

SEM maintains several advantages over simpler analytic techniques such as regression. First, SEM was created to test and refine theoretical models attempting to explain or predict social or behavioral phenomena (Bentler, 1988) and, thus, the method is most appropriate for use in this study. Second, unlike older techniques which assume zero measurement error in sample data (which is never the case), SEM is unique in its ability to isolate measurement error variance during analyses. Third, SEM helps control for inflation of experimentwise (or Type I) error and, lastly, SEM "best honors the [complex] reality to which the researcher is purportedly trying to generalize" (Thompson 1994, p. 12). In health and sexual behavior research, most outcomes (i.e., behaviors) have multiple causes (i.e., predictors) and most causes have multiple outcomes, all interacting dynamically. Researchers in these fields investigate multivariate, not univariate, or isolated, phenomena with only one or two determinants. It is impossible to assess how multiple variables behave in each other's company when a researcher limits an analysis to a univariate/bivariate examination. Instead, SEM allows all variables—multiple independent and dependent variables—to be examined *simultaneously*. (Buhi, Goodson, Neilands, & Blunt, 2011, p. 65)

EXERCISE 33—PRESENT THE LITERATURE REVIEW

TIME NEEDED: 15 minutes x session

MATERIALS NEEDED: Timer; the sources you will cite (your reviewed literature)

The manner in which authors write the literature review portion in an article or grant proposal varies according to the field of study, each writer's style, the journal's style, and the instructions for the grant proposal. Therefore, there are no formulas, no rigid rules for how to write the literature review.[2]

In the absence of strict guidelines, what might be a good way to practice sharpening the presentation of your literature review? Practicing this week's exercise can help: It provides template sentences you can complete and apply to your writing. Spend each practice session this week completing the sentences below. These sentences will help you focus the literature review on the evidence supporting your point, your problem, your approach, or your hypothesis:

☐ These are the studies/reports that **support** (or validate) my **problem, research question, or hypothesis to be tested:** _____ (compile all citations lending support to your *topic*). These studies/reports agree my problem (research question or hypothesis) is worth studying/exploring, *because* _____.

☐ These are the studies/reports that **contradict** the importance of my **problem, research question, or hypothesis to be tested:** _____ (compile all citations disagreeing that your *topic* is worthy of study or deserves testing). These studies/reports disagree that the topic I chose should be examined *because* _____.

☐ These are the studies/reports that **support** (or validate) **the purpose** of my article (or grant proposal): _____ (compile all citations supporting your *purpose*). These studies/reports lend validity to my purpose (or approach, or what I'm proposing to do in this piece), *because* _____.

☐ The sources (citations) that **carry the most authority**, regarding the problem, topic, research question, or approach I'm taking are these: _____ (compile all the citations carrying the greatest weight, the ones holding the most *authority* in your field). The reason(s) they carry such authority is _____.

☐ In my literature review, ___ (number) citations may be considered *dated* or old; on the other hand, ___ (number) citations are *recent*. (Note: If you have too many dated citations, check whether this may represent a problem for the article or grant reviewers, and address the problem appropriately.) The definition for *dated* depends on each academic field's traditions and expectations. Ask your colleagues or professors about it.

EXERCISE 34—LAY OUT THE THEORETICAL FRAMEWORK

TIME NEEDED: 15 minutes x session

MATERIALS NEEDED: Timer; the sources for your theoretical approach or framework

Not all publications or grant proposals in the social sciences present, discuss, or even adopt a theoretical framework for the piece being written. As someone who teaches health behavior theories and has authored a book on theory for health promotion research and practice, I must confess that I tend to be drawn to articles or proposals that *do have* a theoretical perspective. It is like an appropriate frame placed around a beautifully painted canvas. It just completes the picture; it provides the paper a more refined and finished look and helps the argument, the rationale, and the proposed topic stand out! (Not to mention the contribution the study can make to theory development in that particular field.)

Again, it would go beyond the scope of this book to teach you how to develop a theoretical framework or even to advocate for the use of theories. Here, I want to provide ways to *practice* presenting a theoretical framework to readers.

This exercise, therefore, will "force" you to write something about the theoretical framework (a single theory or multiple theories) informing your research, your study, your writing (when applicable, of course; some manuscripts are atheoretical). During each of your practice sessions this week, complete one or more of the following sentences. If you don't know how to complete them, you may need to read or research further into the topic you've chosen. If your manuscript or proposal does not adopt a theory or theoretical frame, skip to Exercise 35.

☐ The theory (or theories) I plan to use as a framework for, or to inform my study, are _____.

☐ These theories were proposed and developed by _____ (provide original sources for the theories' main proponents).

☐ The *sources* I want to cite for the theories are _____, *because* _____.

☐ I chose these particular theories *because* _____. (Note: Explain, in a brief statement, how the theories you chose relate to your subject. Make the link explicit; don't expect the reader[s] to *infer* the relationship between the theories and your topic.)

☐ Originally, each theory was developed (or designed) to explain _____. (Note: Briefly explain the original, intended purpose of each theory.)

☐ Other studies that have applied these theories are _____.

☐ If my use of the theory (or theories) is unconventional and has not been attempted before, why do I believe it's important to use this approach here? _____.

☐ The constructs I will use in my study/report are the following: _____.

☐ If I'm adapting existing theories to my study, my adaptation consists of _____. (Note: Briefly describe how you adapted certain constructs or relationships from the theories for your own purposes.)

EXERCISE 35—CHECK IT

TIME NEEDED: 10 minutes x session

MATERIALS NEEDED: Timer; draft of your introduction

This week, you will practice systematically checking the draft of your introduction (purpose statement, rationale, literature review, and theoretical framework). Go through each question in the checklist below and answer honestly those that apply to your piece. If you sense certain segments need more work (either generating new text or editing), tackle the problem right then: Either spend time generating/editing, or make a note to yourself, in the text, to return to that portion to add or rewrite.

Dedicate 10 minutes per writing session to the checklist below. If you find you need more time, that's okay, but don't binge and dedicate your entire writing session to the checklist. Keep in mind you risk burning out and not wanting to return to your text if you binge write.

Checklist for Introductions[3]

- ☐ Is the problem, topic, research question, or hypothesis I propose to address presented clearly? Can readers outside my field easily identify what I'm proposing to do, even if they do not understand my subject area well?
- ☐ Is the importance of my topic, problem, or research question evident to the reader? Can readers outside my field identify my rationale, even if they cannot understand the specific arguments or available data?
- ☐ Does my introduction contain a clear purpose statement or a sentence beginning with "The purpose of this paper/grant is . . ."?
- ☐ Does my introduction contain any unnecessary information? Can I delete it?
- ☐ Do I cite sources to support my problem (research question, topic, or hypothesis)?
- ☐ Do I cite sources that contradict the importance of my problem/topic (alternative points of view)? Am I being fair in presenting the alternative arguments?
- ☐ Do I cite authoritative sources from my field of study?
- ☐ Do I cite recently published literature?
- ☐ Does my literature review show I know the most important and relevant sources regarding my topic (published as well as unpublished)?
- ☐ Is my literature biased exclusively toward my field? Many topics have been studied by different disciplines, yet we often tend to confine our reading to our particular area. For example, adolescent pregnancy prevention is a popular topic in the public health and pediatric medicine literature, but it has also been studied in the fields of economics and law. Does my literature review provide evidence I have tried to avoid paradigmatic biases (when appropriate)?

□ Do my citations include secondary sources (e.g., "Jones, 1939, as cited in Smith, 1950"). (Note: If you're using secondary citations, be careful. Some fields view the practice of quoting secondary sources as problematic. As much as possible, cite the original references.)

□ Are all the citations I present *necessary?* Does each one contribute to the text, or are some redundant? If redundant, what can I delete? (Note: Remember that citations—even the numbered formats—add to your text's word count. Some journals limit the citations the author[s] may include, due to page restrictions.)

□ Are the citations helpful to the readers? Will they be able to learn something if they check these citations themselves?

□ Am I citing or using other authors' materials, for which I need permission to publish? (Note: If you are using a table, figure, photo, or diagram from another publication, you need to ask for permission from the publisher holding the copyright to that piece. Ensure your use of citations is covered by copyright laws' "fair use" clause.)

□ Is my theoretical framework presented logically and clearly? Could I add a graph or figure to help readers visualize the relationships among the variables in my study?

□ Do I provide enough background about the theory (or theories) I chose to use, to orient readers who are not familiar with the framework?

Notes

1. Grant proposals for federal agencies such as the National Institutes of Health and the National Science Foundation ask for a one-page, all-inclusive synopsis of the proposal labeled the "specific aims" section. That section must contain the following elements: (a) a "catchy" introductory sentence, (b) brief description of current knowledge, (c) the gap in the knowledge base about the topic, (d) the long-term goal for the project, (e) the objective, (f) the central hypothesis, (g) one to three specific aims the proposal plans to achieve, and (h) expected outcomes (Russell & Morrison, 2009/2010).

2. My students always ask me if I know a good strategy for conducting and organizing literature reviews. It is beyond the scope of this book to teach you how to review the literature in your field, but I would strongly recommend J. Garrard's (2011) *Health Sciences Literature Reviews Made Easy* as a useful resource. In that book, Garrard walks the reader step-by-step through the process of conducting a systematic literature review (i.e., a special type of review that is more rigorous and systematic than the traditional ones). Even if you're doing a traditional literature review, you may benefit from her tips and suggestions, especially the one about using a matrix to organize the literature you are reading.

3. Adapted from Reitt's (1984) article "An Academic Author's Checklist: Essential Questions a Scholar or Scientist Must Ask of Any Manuscript in Preparation—and an Editor or Referee Must Also Consider."

Electronic Sources

About ThinkBuzan. (2011). ThinkBuzan.com. Retrieved from http://www.thinkbuzan .com/uk/company/about

Why mind mapping works: The proof is here. (2011). ThinkBuzan.com. Retrieved from http://www.thinkbuzan.com/uk/articles/mindmappingworks

References

Buhi, E. R., Goodson, P., Neilands, T. B., & Blunt, H. B. (2011). Adolescent sexual abstinence: A test of an integrative theoretical framework. *Health Education & Behavior, 38*(1), 63–79.

Casagrande, J. (2010). *It was the best of sentences, it was the worst of sentences.* New York: Ten Speed Press.

Clark, R. P. (2006). *Writing tools: 50 essential strategies for every writer.* New York: Little, Brown.

Garcia, K. M. (2011). *The impact of college students' life experiences on the various dimensions of wellness: A qualitative study.* Unpublished doctoral dissertation, Texas A&M University, College Station.

Garrard, J. (2011). *Health sciences literature reviews made easy: The matrix method* (3rd ed.). Sudbury, MA: Jones & Bartlett.

Reitt, B. B. (1984). An academic author's checklist: Essential questions a scholar or scientist must ask of any manuscript in preparation—and an editor or referee must also consider. *Scholarly Publishing, 16,* 65–72.

Russell, S. W., & Morrison, D. C. (2009/2010). *The grant application writer's workbook.* Bethesda, MD: National Institutes of Health.

Sax, L. J., Hagedorn, L. S., Arredondo, M., & Dicrisi, F. A., III. (2002). Faculty research productivity: Exploring the role of gender and family-related factors. *Research in Higher Education, 43*(4), 423–446.

Chapter Eight

Exercises for Writing the Methods Section

Summary

Think About It . . .

Say all you have to say in the fewest possible words, or your reader will be sure to skip them; and in the plainest possible words or he will certainly misunderstand them.

John Ruskin (1819–1900)

Think About It . . .

The section on methods, in a journal article or research report, is typically the easiest one to write. It is easier from the standpoint that authors merely *describe* what they did in their research. Description of methods entails less abstract, interpretive work than is required in the introduction, results, or discussion sections. Describing what was done is far easier than making connections, sorting through relevant literature, and selecting among appropriate arguments. For this reason, when writers are stuck or don't feel motivated to tackle the introduction, I recommend they begin by writing about what they *did* in their projects (but don't ignore what I argued for in the previous chapter; I really think it's most productive first to capture all your thoughts about the introduction, if you can).

Keep in mind, however, that writing the methods section in a *grant proposal* represents an altogether different challenge from writing about methods for articles or reports. In grant proposals we don't write about what *was* done but about what *will be* done. When we write

---

Research Shows . . .

In 2002, Claire Baldwin and Genevieve E. Chandler described a strategy for promoting faculty writing in a school of nursing: hiring a writing coach to facilitate faculty writing.

Grounding their case study in a solid theoretical framework, the authors explained the value of coaching as a mentoring strategy within organizations. The authors then described the hiring of a non-nursing writing coach (with 25 years of experience writing and publishing "biochemistry and neurochemistry basic research"; p. 11). Faculty used the coach's services voluntarily. The coach met individually with faculty, providing various types of social support, such as emotional, instrumental, informational, and appraisal support.

In terms of outcomes, the authors documented the following:

- Over a period of 2.5 years, 16 of 26 faculty used the coach's services.

- These 16 faculty submitted 21 manuscripts for publication (15 were accepted).

- Faculty who provided feedback emphasized the coaching strategy was "supportive, encouraging, and helpful" (p. 13).

grant proposals, the methods have not yet been applied (save when we are replicating those used in a pilot study). Added to the difficulty of writing with precision about something you haven't yet done is the challenge to stay within the word or page limits determined by the funding agency. For instance, the National Institutes of Health (NIH) restricts the "Research Strategy" section, containing the study's design and methods, to 12 pages for the R01 funding mechanism and 6 pages for the R03 funding mechanism.[1]

Regardless of the type of writing you're presently working on, the exercises below will help you focus on providing the details describing your research design and data collection strategies. To facilitate communication, I will again assume you are writing a journal article or a research report. When applicable, I will mention specific elements grant writers can use to practice the exercise in ways more appropriate to their proposal-writing task.

EXERCISE 36—PRACTICE DESCRIBING

TIME NEEDED: 10 minutes x session

MATERIALS NEEDED: Timer; one or two pictures/photos (from magazines, the Internet, or your personal collection)

Because *description* is the type of writing you will use in the methods section, it is important you tell the reader about all the constructs, the measures, and the steps you took to collect data, in as much detail and as accurately as possible. Keep in mind, the methods section spells out the recipe you used in your project so other researchers—if they wish to replicate your findings—can do so by following your description. Therefore, this exercise forces you to practice *describing* what you see, accurately and in detail. You will practice describing visual images (instead of tables depicting results or statistical tests) because such practice will stretch your description skills. Because you are forced to write descriptively about images, you will find yourself slowing down and paying attention to details. Slowing down and paying attention will serve you well when you describe for your readers the research strategies you used (and, later, your results).

1. Choose an attractive picture from a magazine, newspaper, the Internet, or your personal photo albums. Place it where you can see it while you write.

2. Set your timer for 5 minutes. During these 5 minutes, dump all that comes to your mind as you describe the picture to your readers: Provide as many details as you can about shapes, colors, positions, lighting, proportions, and sizes (for details about dumping, see Chapter 2, Exercise 3 and Chapter 7, Exercise 30). Provide additional details that might not be easy to see but can be inferred, such as smells, texture, weight, speed, and sounds.

3. Once the timer goes off, set it for another 5 minutes. Use the time to clean up the material you generated. Edit the text to make it as clear as possible.

4. Once your time is up, leave the exercise, start your routine writing session, and apply your efforts to describe with precision and accuracy.

During the next practice sessions, repeat the exercise by returning to the original picture: Provide additional description, more details. Ask yourself, "What did I leave out? What is absolutely necessary for the reader to know?" Then, clean your text, aiming for precision, clarity, and brevity. Ask yourself, "What can be cut? What is redundant or unnecessary?"

If you exhaust the description of one picture, choose another one and continue to practice. I challenge you, however, to stick with a single picture and attempt to describe it in different ways. For this, it might help you to imagine having different readers. How would you describe the picture to students in a second-grade classroom? How about to students in a college classroom? And how would your description be worded if senior citizens in a community recreation center were your audience? How would you express it if your readers were professionals in your field?

As you begin to tailor your description to various audiences, think about the elements that need emphasizing and those that may be ignored, depending on the target audience. Remember: You should keep your audience in mind throughout your entire piece, not only in the methods section. It is just a bit easier to *practice* writing in different ways when you're writing descriptively, which is why I'm recommending you practice it here.

Tip for ESL Writers

Descriptive writing appears to be a term requiring no explanation. However, what might constitute description in one culture (or language) may not be the same as in another language/culture.

In English academic writing the term *descriptive* has a specific meaning. In this type of writing, descriptions include *objective* statements that correspond, as much as possible, to what the writer observes or sees. Descriptive writing in academic English avoids *subjective* words, comments, feelings, or impressions.

For example, if you were describing data collection conducted at a school, you would use active verbs depicting the actions/tasks you observed or saw. You might write something such as, "The second-graders examined three pictures the researcher presented to them. After examining the pictures, the researcher asked each child to select the picture they wanted to talk about." This would be considered an objective description. The following sentences, however, would *not* be considered descriptive, given all the subjective terms the writer uses: "The **very young** second-graders examined three **interesting** pictures the researcher presented to them. After the children **spent a lot more time than planned** examining the pictures, the researcher asked each child to select the picture they wanted to talk about." Notice that the words in bold represent the writer's subjective judgments of what happened. Due to these subjective terms, these sentences would not be acceptable as descriptive writing within academic English.

EXERCISE 37—DESCRIBE THE RESEARCH DESIGN

TIME NEEDED: 10 minutes x session

MATERIALS NEEDED: Timer

The research design is the *plan* you developed and followed in your study. More often than not, designs have labels such as *experimental, survey design,* or *emergent design,* which describe the type of data collected and the procedures for collecting them. It is important, therefore, to begin by orienting your reader regarding the big-picture approach to your research study. Did you employ a quantitative, qualitative, or mixed-methods approach? Within each approach or paradigm, specific strategies have specific labels. For instance, a mixed-method study can employ a concurrent design using nested samples, whereas a quantitative study may employ a randomized control trial design (Collins, Onwuegbuzie, & Jiao, 2006; Creswell, 1998).

During this week's practice sessions, describe the research design you chose. If you want to increase your report's quality and credibility, also tell the reader *why* you chose a particular design or why that design is the most appropriate choice for studying your topic (see the discussion about writing rationales in Chapter 7, Exercise 32).

1. Begin by dumping thoughts regarding the design you chose and the rationale for having chosen it. If your choice of design is unique or has never been used before with this topic, this population, or this setting, make sure you mention its uniqueness in the introduction and repeat it in the methods section (there is nothing wrong with strongly emphasizing the innovation your piece offers!). When restating the idea that your study is unique, try to reword your statements so you don't sound boringly repetitive.

2. Use a few sessions this week just to dump what's on your mind. Use the remaining sessions to clean up and edit your description.

3. As you dump, try completing the following sentences (and then adapt them to your text):

   ☐ The research design I employed in the study was . . .
   ☐ I chose this design *because* . . .
   ☐ Employing this research design represents an innovation in the field *because* . . . [if the design represents a new, unique approach to the topic]
   ☐ The design I chose represents the most appropriate approach for this project *because* . . .

If you are writing a grant proposal, don't forget these sentences should be worded in the future tense: "The research design I will employ in this study is . . ." In a proposal you are offering a plan to be carried out in the future, whereas in a research report or journal article you are describing what was done in the past. Keep these tenses in mind.

EXERCISE 38—DESCRIBE THE SAMPLE

TIME NEEDED: 10 minutes x session

MATERIALS NEEDED: Timer

Whether your study's sample comprised human beings, animals, historical documents, artifacts, or even published journal articles—as in a meta-analysis or systematic literature review—some elements are common to all descriptions:

- ☐ The sample's size—how many?
- ☐ Statistical power: Does this sample give your study adequate statistical power to find modest or strong relationships among the variables you're measuring?
- ☐ Size of sample's subgroups: If there were groups in the sample, how many in each group? (e.g., how many girls and how many boys in the sixth-grade classes you surveyed?)
- ☐ The sample's characteristics: What *kinds* of documents, animals, or people did you include in your sample? (e.g., were different ethnic groups represented in your sample of college students?)
- ☐ Your rationale for choosing this particular sample (this age group, these journals): Why did you choose *this* sample and not another?
- ☐ Sample recruitment (or how did you obtain your sample?): Describe the strategies employed to get people to participate in your study or the techniques you used to access the documents you reviewed.

This week's exercise, therefore, requires that you:

1. Dump and edit everything you can think of related to the sample in your study, for 10 minutes every session.

2. Follow the checklist above to guide *what* you write about.

3. Recall the level of detail you employed when practicing Exercise 36. In this exercise, also, try to describe your sample in as much detail as possible. You can always edit out unnecessary details later, when you tailor the manuscript to conform to the instructions regarding word/page limits. For now, add as much as possible; paint as vivid and clear a word picture as you possibly can of who (or what artifacts) took part in your study.

EXERCISE 39—DESCRIBE THE MEASURES

TIME NEEDED: 10 minutes x session

MATERIALS NEEDED: Timer

Qualitative studies don't concern themselves with *measuring* what is being studied. Therefore, this section may not be very useful for authors writing strictly qualitative reports. For qualitative researchers, the investigator *is the instrument* and is expected to interact with the data being collected—a stark contrast to quantitative inquiry, which requires the researcher to maintain a certain distance from the data. Qualitative researchers, therefore, concern themselves with capturing trustworthy data, while quantitative researchers strive to capture valid and reliable data, or data measured with as much precision as possible (Lincoln & Guba, 1985).

Concerns with the quality of measuring tools and their ability to yield valid and reliable data are, therefore, central to quantitative or mixed-methods studies. Accurately describing the measures and tools employed is essential to establish the study's internal validity or accuracy. Accurate description is also required for future replication of that research project.

As you describe your measures in the methods section, keep in mind what Zinsser (1988) tells us about writing "visible detail." It may help guide you through the description process:

> Writing is not unlike the schoolroom period called "show and tell." The writer should not only tell a story: he should try to make the reader *see* what he is writing about . . . active verbs are ideal for this kind of work: they force us to witness an event. (p. 72)

Zinsser's message is simple: Help the reader visualize the strategies, the measures, and the tools you used. Do this by using *active* verbs and by avoiding the passive voice. For example, try to write this:

> Participants in our study filled out the Beck Depression Inventory. The Inventory consists of 21 items designed to measure self-reported depression states. (Beck, Ward, Mendelson, Mock, & Erbaugh, 1961)

Instead of this:

> The Beck Depression Inventory was utilized as the measure for depression. The inventory was developed with 21 questions, designed to measure self-reported depression states.

The exercise this week will focus on measures as they are used in quantitative or mixed-methods studies. It follows the pattern of the previous exercises:

1. Dump and clean, generate and edit your text regarding the measures used in your study, for 10 minutes every writing session this week. Your goal: to describe, in as much detail as possible, the tools you employed to measure or collect your data.

2. As you generate text, make sure to address the elements listed below (if applicable to your type of study). Focus on one or two items from the list in each practice session this week. Avoid writing *everything* about the measures in a single session. To ensure you capture all the details, focus on only one or two during each session.
   ☐ How are you measuring the variables in your study? Which measures are you using?
   ☐ Did you develop your own measurement instruments or did you use someone else's? Did you adapt your measurement instrument from a specific source? Provide the appropriate reference/citation for that source.
   ☐ Your reasons for having chosen *these* measures over others: What makes these measures the most appropriate for your study?
   ☐ If the way in which you used certain measures is entirely unique, how does this uniqueness contribute significantly to the literature in your field?
   ☐ If using different types of measures in the same study (for instance, anxiety scales alongside blood pressure readings), make sure you describe and provide the rationale for choosing each one.
   ☐ Describe each measure in detail: How many items or questions does it have? What does the measuring instrument look like?
   ☐ Discuss the instrument's calibration: Does it generate valid and reliable data? Have others used it successfully? Provide citations for these uses, when applicable.
   ☐ What evidence do *you* have, using data from *your* study, that these measures can generate reliable and valid information? (Notice I don't talk about valid or reliable *instruments,* because validity and reliability are characteristics of the *data,* not of the measurement tool—for more on this topic, see Thompson, 2003.)
   ☐ Have your measures been pretested with the sample in your study? If so, describe the pretesting and its findings in detail. Remember: At this point, describe only what you found about the quality or performance of the measures; do not describe what you found in terms of your research question or hypothesis. That will come later.
   ☐ Are there limitations in the measurements you're using (or *will use,* if you're writing a grant proposal?). If so, list them now. Later you may choose to describe these limitations more fully, in the limitations section at the end of your manuscript. Grant proposals usually have designated sections to discuss the problems you foresee in your study, along with their potential solutions. If the measures may represent a problem, discuss this now, while you are thinking about it.

EXERCISE 40—DESCRIBE DATA COLLECTION AND DATA MANAGEMENT PROCEDURES

TIME NEEDED: 10 minutes x session

MATERIALS NEEDED: Timer

As you already know, describing how you collected and managed your data constitutes an important section in your article/report because it will provide the details other researchers need to replicate the study correctly or judge its validity. More often than not, however, data collection and management procedures are relegated to a few sentences, such as:

Data collection occurred between January and December of 2010. The data were stored in a computer database for analysis.

These sentences lack detail regarding, for instance, how frequently the researchers collected data throughout the year and whether data collection occurred at a regular pace (equal number of interviews conducted each month, for example) or in spurts (a lot done in January, then quite a bit more in July, and a final push in December). The author says nothing about how he/she processed or managed the data from the moment they were obtained until the moment they were ready for analysis. If the data came from audio recordings of interviews, how were the recordings utilized? Did someone transcribe them? Did respondents check the transcripts for accuracy? Such details are important for replication.

Granted, there is never enough room in a journal manuscript, or even in a grant proposal, to describe *all* these details. Nevertheless, you should capture them now, during your practice sessions, so you can proactively decide which details can be safely omitted because they're not crucial for replicating the study and which ones *must* be included. You can make this decision only when you have most details in front of you. The alternative is to omit important details unintentionally because you wrote the methods section at the last minute, under a deadline, with no time to check your description for accuracy.

To describe in detail how you conducted each step in the study requires using active verbs denoting action, movement, and tasks. The exercise this week focuses on developing a list of active verbs you can use and then using them to describe the steps you took in your study.

1. Each day, set your timer for 5 minutes and brainstorm a few active verbs you might use to describe collecting and managing your data. If necessary, use a thesaurus to see what options are available for verbs such as *collected, managed,* and *stored* (see Chapter 6, Exercise 24 for how to practice using a thesaurus as well as a reverse dictionary). For example, here are some active verbs you can use to describe the tasks occurring during data collection in some types of studies:

Amass	Accumulate
Store	Bundle
Assemble	Cluster
Lump together	Collate
Aggregate	Compile
Associate	Conglomerate
Gather	Convene
Reassemble	Draw (from)
Bring together	Obtain
Pile	Pack
Group	Unite

Also, authors Rebecca K. Frels, Anthony J. Onwuegbuzie, and John R. Slate (2010) have published a useful "typology of verbs representing knowledge or action for scholarly writing." You may want to get ahold of this typology and practice applying the verbs they have listed.

2. When your timer beeps, reset it for another 5 minutes and dump all you can remember about the activities that went on during the data collection and data management phases in your study. Try to use as many of the verbs you listed as possible.

3. During your next practice sessions, repeat the exercise, devoting half the time to generating a list of active verbs and the other half to dumping and cleaning your description. During the dumping and cleaning, make it a point to use as many listed active verbs as you can.

4. The list below will help focus your dumping a bit more, when you dump and clean during this week's practice sessions. If nothing else, the list will stimulate your thinking about the specific steps you took in the study. Describe one or two elements from the list below, in as much detail as possible. Apply as many action verbs from your list as you can.

☐ What were the steps I (we) took to collect the data? Step 1: . . . ; Step 2: . . .

☐ How long did it take to collect each data point (total time spent collecting data from one person, animal, tissue, or journal article)? How long did the data collection take, overall (total time spent collecting data)?

☐ What happened to the data once they were collected? How were they stored, transported, and accessed by the author(s) for analysis?

☐ Were qualitative data sent back to participants for accuracy checking?

☐ If the study involved human subjects, how did you obtain informed consent (if applicable)?

☐ If the study was qualitative and involved transcribing interviews, who transcribed? Who developed field notes and how were they managed?

☐ Did the data need cleaning? How did you manage the cleaning phase?

This list is by no means exhaustive or applicable to all types of studies. But even if not useful in its entirety, it will help trigger your memory regarding the important details you need to include when describing your methods.

EXERCISE 41—DESCRIBE THE DATA ANALYSIS

TIME NEEDED: 10 minutes x session

MATERIALS NEEDED: Timer

This week's exercise will help you practice writing about your data analysis. Use the dump-and-clean method for 10 minutes each practice session. Focus on one element from the list below, and write everything you can think of about your analysis—capturing as much detail as you can now remember or gather from old notes.

1. If you analyzed your data **quantitatively** (or used statistical techniques), answer these questions:

   ☐ Missing data: How did you manage them? Did you check the data for patterns of "missingness" (Buhi, Goodson, & Neilands, 2008)? How did you solve the missing-data problem, if it occurred? What does the reader need to know about how you handled the missing data in your study?

   ☐ Statistical techniques: Which strategies (statistical tests, counts, structural models, effect size measures) did you use to analyze your data?

   ☐ Your rationale: Why did you choose these particular analytical strategies and not others? (e.g., why did you choose to conduct an ANCOVA instead of a multiple regression analysis?)

   ☐ What sources (other authors, similar studies, classical texts) might support your analysis choice? Can you cite them? Would citing them add validity to your study?

   ☐ Are your readers familiar with the data analysis you conducted in your study, or will you need to educate your audience (briefly) about the technique? How much do they need to know to be able to understand the analysis?

   ☐ Did you run alternative analyses to check the validity of your findings? If you did, are you letting your readers know about it? In how much detail?

2. If you analyzed your data **qualitatively,** answer these questions:

   ☐ Which analytical strategies did you employ?

   ☐ What sources (other authors, similar studies, or classical texts) might support your choice of analysis? Can you cite them? Would citing them add validity to your study?

   ☐ Could your data have been analyzed through a different approach or analytical strategy? If so, why did you opt for this one?

   ☐ What steps did you take in the data analysis process? (e.g., did you segment the written transcripts by paragraphs, sentences, or words?)

☐ How did you develop the codes for a thematic data analysis? Did you come up with your own code labels? Did you borrow, verbatim, from participants' words, or did you use an existing theory's constructs as labels?

☐ How did you combine common themes or ideas?

☐ Did you develop or use a codebook to analyze your data?

☐ How many people analyzed the data? Did you have an analytical team? Did you check for interrater reliability? If so, will you report it?

☐ In the case of interviews, did participants check the accuracy of the transcribed data?

☐ Did you perform any sort of counting or numerical analysis of your qualitative data? If so, have you described to your readers what you did?

Note

1. R01 and R03 designate different types of grants for which researchers can apply within the NIH. R01s award more money and require preliminary (pilot) data. R03s are smaller grants that, in most cases, don't require the researcher to present pilot data.

References

Baldwin, C., & Chandler, G. E. (2002). Improving faculty publication output: The role of a writing coach. *Journal of Professional Nursing, 18*(1), 8–15.

Beck, A. T., Ward, C. H., Mendelson, M., Mock, J., & Erbaugh, J. (1961, June). An inventory for measuring depression. *Archives of General Psychiatry, 4*, 53–63.

Buhi, E. R., Goodson, P., & Neilands, T. B. (2008). Out of sight, not out of mind: Strategies for handling missing data. *American Journal of Health Behavior, 32*(1), 83–92.

Collins, K. M. T., Onwuegbuzie, A. J., & Jiao, Q. G. (2006). Prevalence of mixed-methods sampling designs in social science research. *Evaluation and Research in Education, 19*(2), 83–101.

Creswell, J. W. (1998). *Qualitative inquiry and research design: Choosing among five traditions.* Thousand Oaks: Sage.

Frels, R. K., Onwuegbuzie, A. J., & Slate, J. R. (2010). Editorial: A typology of verbs for scholarly writing. *Research in the Schools, 17*(1), xx–xxxi.

Lincoln, Y., & Guba, E. G. (1985). *Naturalistic inquiry.* Newbury Park, CA: Sage.

Thompson, B. (Ed.). (2003). *Score reliability: Contemporary thinking on reliability issues.* Thousand Oaks, CA: Sage.

Zinsser, W. (1988). *Writing to learn: How to write—and think—clearly about any subject at all.* New York: Harper & Row.

Chapter Nine

Exercises for Writing the Results/Findings Section

Summary

Think About It . . .

EXERCISE 42—Picture the Findings

EXERCISE 43—Describe Most Important Findings

Checklist for Results/Findings Sections

EXERCISE 44—Summarize Least Important Findings

Don't tell me the moon is shining; show me the glint of light on broken glass.

Anton Chekhov (1860–1904)

Think About It . . .

The results or findings section in your journal article constitutes the heart and soul of your research report. In this section you bring the reader to a convergence point: the place where all the threads presented throughout the introduction and the methods sections finally connect. Findings/results represent your chance to arrive and shine, so write this section well!

After those long, tedious months analyzing data and all that boring time when getting new toner for the printer was your most exciting accomplishment, you have your findings: all the outcomes of your thematic analyses, all the results from the statistical tests and numerical calculations. Such an exciting moment! It is much like having a baby: You experience such exhilaration and all the pain and labor fade rather quickly.

Like any proud parent, however, you want everyone to see all the details in this product of yours: the tiny hands, the wee-little toes. You know . . . *everything.* So you take pictures—hundreds of them!

Research Shows . . .

Elizabeth Creamer (1995) interviewed 23 faculty women in 1994. All women worked at doctorate-granting institutions in the mid-Atlantic area and had earned doctoral degrees in education. Of the 23 interviewees, 19 were classified as "highly productive writers: those who had published five or more articles in the last two years or twenty or more articles cumulatively" (p. 3). Creamer asked her interviewees to discuss "how four factors contributed to their ability to do scholarly writing: personal qualities, graduate program [graduate training], organizational and institutional supports, and participation in professional associations" (p. 4).

Of special interest are the findings in the categories *personal qualities* and *graduate program.* Regarding *personal qualities,* Creamer states, "few [interviewees] described writing as something that comes easily or naturally to them. The majority reported they have developed highly personalized routines that enable them to 'carve out' time for writing over extended periods of time. Capturing the arduousness of the process, one participant said, 'Do I like writing? I like it when I have finished writing'" (p. 4).

In the category *graduate program,* Creamer writes: "Although most of the women became faculty, few indicated that their doctoral programs provided the skills they needed for research and scholarly publication" (pp. 5–6).

We react the same way when finally we birth the results or findings from a research study. Like proud parents, we, too, want to report every single little detail of what we found (look, girls outperformed boys in our study, even though we weren't even looking for differences between genders!). We forget, however: People quickly tire after seeing picture #213 of a sleeping baby. While we believe each and every finding is extremely important, our readers want only the bottom line, the take-home message from our study. They quickly lose interest when overwhelmed with mounds of irrelevant information.

Therefore, the KEY to writing a fruitful and outstanding results/findings section is to write *selectively.* According to Paul J. Silvia (2007):

> The *Results* section describes your analyses. Beginning writers feel compelled to report every possible analysis of their data, probably because thesis and dissertation committees want to see such analyses. Journal articles should be crisp: Report only the results that bear on your problem. Bad results sections are long lists of numbers and statistical tests; *good results sections create a story.* (p. 86; emphasis added)

The exercises below will help you practice telling a good story using only selected results. Remember, however: Some grant proposals ask for anticipated findings or expected results. In this case, it may be even more important to weave the results/findings into an interesting story, even though you may have to predict or envision them at this point.[1]

EXERCISE 42—PICTURE THE FINDINGS

TIME NEEDED: 15 minutes x session

MATERIALS NEEDED: Timer; a print-out or a list of your findings/results

During each practice session this week, you will spend your time "picturing" the findings from your study. Having a visual representation of your results will make writing about them far, far easier than you anticipated. More often than not, writers skip this step, creating the visual depictions of their data *after* they have written the results section. I recommend you BEGIN with the charts, tables, figures, drawings, diagrams, or photographs. After you've developed these visuals, write about them.

Your exercise this week, therefore, will involve spending time being creative:

1. Choose the findings you believe are the most important in your study (or, if you want, begin with the easiest-to-understand findings).

2. Search for creative ways to display them in tables, figures, pictures, diagrams, or photographs. You may already have computer print-outs of statistical tests in tables, which you will merely copy and paste into your paper. I recommend you redesign those tables and find ways to pack in more information per visual than your average statistical software will.

3. Develop three to four good visuals, representing your *most important* findings.

4. Schedule time with someone you trust to obtain feedback on the visuals. You should check whether they communicate clearly or need improvement.

5. Spend each practice session this week developing these visuals and scheduling meeting times to obtain feedback.

6. Keep your feedback appointments and consider the feedback you receive on your graphs, tables, or figures as seriously as you would consider the feedback on your written drafts.

Moreover, while developing the graphs and tables for your findings, keep in mind: A picture is worth a thousand words—always! Therefore—especially in those cases where you have limited page or word counts—*spend time* creating the most compelling, attractive, and informative visuals for your study as you possibly can!

Most academic authors think of tables, graphs, and charts as another media or another way to report the data they have already described in words. Many authors forget, however, that representing data visually can be much more than just a reporting medium. Visuals can also function as *data analysis tools*. How so? Graphs, charts, tables, and figures help you perceive *patterns* in the findings. Some patterns you won't be able to recognize by merely writing about your data. Identifying unique patterns in the findings will help you tell the interesting story you want to tell. Only visual depictions can make these patterns jump out and become clear.

Therefore, instead of using visuals to complement or illustrate a story you're telling in the text, consider writing the text as a complement to the story being told by the visuals. Develop the visual aids first, see what patterns emerge, *and then* write *that* story you see in the graphs. You will have a much richer and more interesting story to tell. It will also be more fun to write!

In order to develop these creative visuals, you need to spend time with your findings. As you design them, you will also get a better sense of which findings you need to report and which don't belong in this piece. In other words, you will refine your perception of which findings are the most relevant and which are least important. This distinction will prepare you for next week's exercises.

If you need resources to help develop interesting visuals, there are several instructive books and websites available. Take a look at the resources listed in the Appendix. One of the most exciting visualization efforts I came across recently was developed by a foundation called Gapminder (see http://www.gapminder.org/). Granted, their tools are better suited for presentations than for print media, but they may inspire you to create and explore new ways to display your data using computer technology.

EXERCISE 43—DESCRIBE MOST IMPORTANT FINDINGS

TIME NEEDED: 15 minutes x session

MATERIALS NEEDED: Timer; the visuals (graphs, tables, figures, charts) developed last week

Spend 15 minutes in each practice session writing *about* the visuals you developed last week. Notice that I didn't say *write the data from your tables*. Instead, I said, write ABOUT your visuals. Generate text describing the *patterns* emerging from your visuals but not every detail. As Wendy L. Belcher (2009) says in *Writing Your Journal Article in 12 Weeks:*

> Don't pack a sentence with a list of percentages. Let the tables work for you; that is what they are there for. Use the text to *point out trends* in the tables or highlight the significance of some of the most interesting data; do not repeat the data. (p. 194; emphasis added)

The key words in Belcher's quote are *trends* and *interesting*. Pay attention to them.

You may begin this week's exercise without necessarily having made all the decisions about which findings you will report and which you will move to another article. These decisions will mature as *you write* about your findings. Just select a few findings you believe are most important and focus on those. Begin writing about them now; as you write, you will come to final decisions rather intuitively. Your writing will guide your choices if you practice these steps:

1. Set your timer for 15 minutes.

2. Choose one of the visuals you developed last week.

3. Write freely, capturing all your thoughts about the findings in that single graph. Don't be afraid to include any questions you might be asking of these findings (what might they mean?)—you will use these thoughts later, when writing the *discussion* section. Capture all the associations that come to mind while you write (e.g., "This finding is very, very similar to the one in Jones's study in 2001; I need to double-check it"). Remember: Your goal is not to have a finished, polished piece right now. The purpose is merely to CAPTURE all your thoughts and all the associations your mind makes related to the findings in that table or graph.

4. Use practice sessions later in the week to edit, polish, and incorporate the bits you wrote during the previous practice sessions into your actual article, report, or grant proposal. Remember to tie each item to your main argument, research question, or hypotheses. You should avoid presenting any findings that do not directly answer the questions/hypotheses proposed in your intro- duction. (Note: One way to decide which are the most important findings is to ask yourself, "Does this particular finding answer the questions I posed in the introduction? Does this finding provide the solution to a specific problem/hypothesis?" If findings do not directly answer your questions or result from testing your hypotheses, they may not be important, at least not important to this report.)

5. As you write your results/findings section, check it against the list below.

Checklist for Results/Findings Sections

☐ Each finding/result contributes to answering a specific question in the manu- script.

☐ Findings are presented in an organized fashion (preferably in the *same order* in which the questions/hypotheses were proposed). Ask yourself whether it is easy to locate your findings within the text (use subheadings to organize). A tip: In the results section, repeat the question or hypothesis proposed origi- nally so readers can remember precisely what you were asking or testing.

☐ Findings are accurate. Calculations have been checked twice; qualitative themes have been checked by more than one coder (interrater reliability), when applicable.

☐ Findings describe the quality of the data being reported (scales' internal con- sistency; content validity and score reliability).

☐ Findings are depicted through interesting and informative visuals, when appropriate.

☐ All visuals depicting findings are mentioned within the text at least once, with a corresponding call-out, such as "See Table 1.1."

☐ Every visual mentioned in the text has its corresponding graph, diagram, or table. Although this sounds redundant, it is important to check: Few things are more frustrating to the reader than looking for a nonexistent graph or table mentioned in the text.

Tip for ESL Writers

Remember Chapter 8, where I alerted ESL writers to the dangers of using words that connote *opinions* or *values* in descriptive writing? Here, too, the same principle applies: While describing the findings from your study, avoid using any *opinion-type* or *value-laden* words.

Here's an example from a manuscript I reviewed recently (I have altered the sentence somewhat to maintain the author's anonymity):

> It is obvious that in this sample, persons with promiscuous sexual behavior also had sexually promiscuous attitudes.

What are the problems in this statement? There are at least two, both related to nondescriptive phrases: first, the use of the word *obvious*. It is the author's job to write and present the findings clearly, but it is inappropriate to assume the results are obvious. In fact, they may be unclear to many readers. *Obvious*, therefore, reflects the author's own opinion about how clearly he/she presented the findings. It is not, however, a descriptive term.

The second problem in this example is the use of the word *promiscuous* to describe sexual relationships with various partners and to qualify a specific type of attitude toward sex. The term *promiscuous* carries a negative connotation. Sex researchers attempt to describe sexual behavior in neutral, scientific terms, and *promiscuous* is as far away from a neutral word as a writer can get: It implies a judgment or condemnation of that particular behavior. The term, therefore, should not be used in academic writing about sexuality. The author should have written something like this, instead:

> In this sample, participants who had sexual relationships with multiple partners also had sexually permissive attitudes. The association was statistically significant at the .01 level of probability.

EXERCISE 44—SUMMARIZE LEAST IMPORTANT FINDINGS

TIME NEEDED: 10 minutes x session

MATERIALS NEEDED: Timer; list of visuals for your study's findings

This week you will spend time practicing summarizing your least important findings.

1. Set your timer for 10 minutes. Examine the visual aids you produced a couple of weeks ago, along with all the study's findings.

2. Choose a few findings you consider not as important and bullet-list them. I know: This may sound funny. You created visuals to depict the less important data, and now I'm telling you to list them in plain text. Yes, because crafting a bulleted list forces you to keep the text concise and your presentation short. If these findings are not very important, you don't want to give them the same weight and attention you gave the most important ones.

3. Once your bulleted list is complete, practice drafting one short paragraph summarizing all the findings you listed. Try to write various versions of this summary. As much as possible, force yourself to describe within a single paragraph all elements in the list (it may not be easy or even possible, but give it a try).

The goal, here, is to have available a brief paragraph touching on these least important findings so your reader will know you detected and considered them. This summary-type paragraph might turn out to be one of those paragraphs essential to your written piece to satisfy reviewers or dissertation committee members or to show you know.

Because you don't want to spend much time or space detailing these findings, practice developing a concise, brief summary. Starting with the bulleted list helps.

Note

1. Whether you should use the term *results* or *findings* varies by academic field and type of study being reported. Personally, I prefer to use *results* when I'm reporting findings from statistical tests or numerical analyses. I reserve the term *findings* for reporting the outcomes from qualitative studies. Findings are uncovered or discovered and, thus, a more appropriate term to describe what happens in qualitative

research using emergent designs (Lincoln & Guba, 1985). Results are products of numerical calculations, typical of quantitative or experimental studies. This preference for using *results* in quantitative studies and *findings* for qualitative studies is merely a matter of personal style; there are no definitive rules here.

Electronic Sources

Gapminder: http://www.gapminder.org/

References

Belcher, W. L. (2009). *Writing your journal article in 12 weeks: A guide to academic publishing success*. Thousand Oaks, CA: Sage.

Creamer, E. (1995). The scholarly productivity of women academics. *Initiatives, 57*(1), 1–9.

Lincoln, Y., & Guba, E. G. (1985). *Naturalistic inquiry*. Newbury Park, CA: Sage.

Silvia, P. J. (2007). *How to write a lot: A practical guide to productive academic writing*. Washington, DC: American Psychological Association.

Chapter Ten

Exercises for Writing the Discussion or Conclusion Section

Summary

Think About It . . .

EXERCISE 45—Question the Results/Findings

EXERCISE 46—Connect the Dots: Other Research

EXERCISE 47—Connect the Dots: Relevant Theory

EXERCISE 48—Guide Your Reader Into the Future

EXERCISE 49—Confess Limitations

The proper force of words lie(s) not in the words themselves, but in their application.

William Hazlitt (1778–1830)

Think About It . . .

We find discussion or conclusion sections at the end of journal articles. Some journals ask for *both* discussions and conclusions; some want one *or* the other. Whether you should have a section labeled *discussion* or one labeled *conclusion* depends on your audience or the journal for which you are writing. Regardless, these final segments of a manuscript accomplish similar purposes—so similar, in fact, many authors view them as interchangeable. My recommendation is this: Investigate what the journal (where you're submitting your manuscript) wants by examining recently published articles, and follow their format.

While grant proposals don't have conclusions and/or discussions, these sections tend to be the most important segments in journal articles (and, often, the most interesting). So it shouldn't surprise us to learn from Belcher (2009) that, given their prominence, they are also "the most difficult section[s] to write" (p. 195).

But wait! If you remember, we said practically the same thing about writing introductions: Authors don't like tackling introductions because they are difficult to write. Now Belcher admits the discussion/conclusion section is the most difficult one . . . so, which is it: the introduction or the discussion?

Before you begin worrying about that, let me warn you: *Both* introduction and discussion/conclusion sections are difficult to write, no matter what. The reasons behind the difficulty may vary, but they are equally difficult and equally significant.

As I wrote in Chapter 7, introductions are important because they have many tasks to accomplish, including furnishing a road map for your readers. But what makes the discussion/conclusion section so important? Simple: its *purpose*—to make sense of all the information you collected and analyzed. It is here that the story about your research comes together. It is in this section that readers will have a chance to see the most interesting part of your story at a quick glance: "what you *thought* would happen, what *did* happen and *why* you think it happened" (Belcher, 2009, p. 195).

The discussion/conclusion section also is important because, often, this is the *only* section within an article that most readers actually read word for word! Many people skip the introduction, methods, and results, heading straight to the discussion, looking for a summary of the most salient findings along with your interpretation of them. Because abstracts describe only what the researcher did—but don't provide detailed interpretations or connections to other studies—readers will first skim through the abstract and then skip to the conclusion/discussion. Here, more than ever, you need tight paragraphs containing the key idea in the first sentence. This terse style helps the reader quickly search the discussion to focus exclusively on its most interesting points.

A well-written discussion/conclusion section, then, summarizes the most salient findings but, above all, *interprets* those findings for the reader. Interpretation involves not only discussing what the findings might mean but also helping the reader think about your findings' *applications* and *implications* for practice or research.

In the beginning of my career I struggled to write conclusion/discussion sections. Honestly, I didn't know what to *say* once I had described my findings. I used to think the findings spoke for themselves. After all, if I could clearly see the implications and what the findings meant . . . wouldn't the readers see them, too? Because I had this attitude and lacked the skills to write a good conclusion, reviewers who read my early manuscripts would always, always (!) criticize my papers for the quality of the discussions: They lacked depth, and, most important, they failed to address my own findings. I would often go on tangents discussing the problem I had examined and would completely neglect talking about *what I found* and *what it might mean.* Consider these comments I received from early reviews:

> The discussion is not tied to findings. For example, the author emphasizes the importance of educating seminary students about family planning, but knowledge seems to have had little impact on the other variables in the model. (Manuscript submitted in 2001)

> This is a well-written paper, but is much too long in some places (e.g., introduction) and too brief in others (e.g., discussion). (Manuscript submitted in 2001)

But I have learned! I've finally learned to write coherent and significant discussions/conclusions. Now reviewers criticize my manuscripts for having discussion sections that are *too* lengthy—I have way too much to say about my findings and way too many dots to connect for my readers.

Oh, yes, I also have learned that readers don't *necessarily* see what I see in my findings or in my data. They may need to be *told or shown* what I see: I spell it out for them because, no, the findings are not self-evident, the implications are not obvious, and the applications I detect are not necessarily the ones they perceive.

How did I learn, you might ask? By reading about how to write conclusions/discussions and by purposefully paying attention to how good writers wrote *their* sections. I also paid close attention to the elements I present in the exercises below. Once I started addressing each of these elements in all my manuscripts, I had more than enough to write in-depth discussions/conclusions that never veered into tangents and always connected closely to my findings.

Research Shows . . .

Daniel Teodorescu (2000) examined the productivity of faculty from 10 countries (Australia, Brazil, Chile, Hong Kong, Israel, Japan, Korea, Mexico, the United Kingdom, and the United States). He defined productivity as the number of articles faculty published in a 3-year period. His goal was to investigate whether the factors influencing faculty productivity in developed countries were similar to those affecting academics in developing countries.

Teodorescu used data from the International Survey of the Academic Profession, collected by the Carnegie Foundation for the Advancement of Teaching, in the United States.

Among his findings were these:

- Factors vary in importance among countries. Age, for instance, was a predictive factor only in the United States.

- Gender "per se does not contribute significantly or meaningfully to the explanation of productivity" (p. 213).

- Time spent on teaching does not impact productivity (with the exception of Japan). According to Teodorescu, "productive scholarship does not appear to be impeded by a devotion to teaching" (p. 215).

- The only factor significantly associated with productivity across all 10 countries is membership in professional societies and attendance at professional conferences.

EXERCISE 45—QUESTION THE RESULTS/FINDINGS

TIME NEEDED: 10 minutes x session

MATERIALS NEEDED: Timer; visuals of your findings/results; what you wrote during Exercise 43 in Chapter 9

Recall Chapter 9, where I recommended—in Exercise 43—that you "write freely, capturing all your thoughts about the findings" and stated, "You will use these thoughts later, when writing the discussion section"? Well, later is now:

1. Set your timer for 10 minutes.

2. Dig through what you wrote during Exercise 43 and look for the thoughts you noted about your findings, especially the *questions* you may have asked about your data.

3. Relist those thoughts in bullet form.

4. During one or two 10-minute practice sessions this week, brainstorm any other questions your findings/results bring up. Bullet-list these questions. During these practice sessions, put on your reader hat and think like your audience: Imagine the questions *they* might have when reading your study for the first time. What might *they* be asking or have interest in? Add these to the bulleted list.

   If you have difficulty generating these questions, ask a colleague to examine your visuals (tables, charts, or figures depicting your findings) and see what kinds of questions they may have. List these questions. Don't worry about answering them right now. Don't even worry about whether they *can* be answered.

5. In subsequent practice or regular writing sessions, begin answering the most intriguing or relevant questions. Begin by answering those connected directly to your purpose statement, to your research question, or to the hypothesis you tested. Ignore the questions that lead you into tangents and connect loosely to your purpose.

   In answering the questions listed, you *interpret* the findings for readers. This is what discussion sections are all about: going a step beyond merely presenting findings (here's what we found) to reflecting on potential meanings (here's why we think we found this).

   However, take note: You should not only *answer* questions your readers might have but should also use this space to *ask* questions of your own. Discussion and conclusion sections are the best place to pose difficult questions to the field, such as "Are we moving in the appropriate direction?" "Should the field continue pursuing this line of inquiry?" and "Are we being ethical in our approach to this topic?" Here is your chance to raise infrequently asked questions or controversial issues and to challenge the field to think differently about a subject.

Example

Consider this excerpt from a manuscript in which my coauthors and I challenged the field of health education. At the time we wrote this article, the field insisted on developing sexuality education programs aimed at changing adolescents' *self-esteem*. After we documented, through a systematic literature review, that "60% of empirical tests of the relationship between self-esteem and adolescents' sexual behavior/attitudes/intentions show no statistically significant associations" (Goodson, Buhi, & Dunsmore, 2006, p. 316), we confronted readers by raising these pointed questions:

> Finally, this review raises the question of *why*—given such lack of supporting evidence—do health promotion and educational programs continue to target self-esteem enhancement as a means to promote healthy decision-making and behavior. Given the absence of empirical data on this issue, perhaps a more fruitful and pressing matter is, instead, whether practitioners' emphasis on self-esteem could be dismissed as innocuous. In other words, is there a problem with health promotion and educational practice continuing to emphasize the improvement of self-esteem? (p. 317)

With these questions we challenged the field to think about two important issues: (a) If there's no support for the practice, why do we continue to develop programs that emphasize adolescents' self-esteem as a risk-protective factor, and (b) is business-as-usual a safe strategy? Although not very popular questions, we believed the field needed to be confronted on the issue, and this section of the manuscript offered the best venue for the challenge.

Discussions and conclusions, then, are *THE* place to contribute to the ongoing dialogue in your field, to raise the difficult questions and motivate the field to answer them. Therefore, be strategic in writing the discussion/conclusion and use the opportunity to influence readers in your field of study.

EXERCISE 46—CONNECT THE DOTS: OTHER RESEARCH

TIME NEEDED: 10 minutes x session

MATERIALS NEEDED: Timer; visuals of your findings/results

It is useful to begin discussion/conclusion sections by summarizing the study's most important findings, providing take-home sound bites of what you found—especially when there are many statistical tests or numerous results. This is the moment to refresh your reader's memory. A short paragraph will do. Concise statements are in order.

Once you've briefly summarized the most important results, it is time to link them to other research: How are your findings similar to or different from the most authoritative studies in your field? Do you confirm the status quo, or do your findings question what has been held as valid thus far? Do your results offer an opportunity for a paradigm shift? If so, you *need* to point that out to readers. Don't expect them to see what is obvious to you. The reader needs your help to capture the big picture, to reach that *aha!* moment you experienced when you were analyzing the data.

When you connect the dots between your study and other published research, you engage in a *discussion*, in a conversation. In this exercise you will practice associating your findings with others (supporting or opposing). The exercise will help you organize your material and systematically discuss what you uncovered in your study so you can contribute to the stimulating conversations happening in your field (Huff, 1999).

1. Set your timer for 10 minutes.

2. During each practice session this week, spend the time listing each salient finding in a separate row of a table or matrix.

3. In a column adjacent to the findings, jot down citations for other research studies that you believe are worth mentioning to the reader because those findings either lend support to or contradict your own.

4. Once you've captured all the other studies to which you want to connect your results, use the next column in the matrix to bullet-list *how* these other studies' findings and yours converge or diverge.

When you finish developing this matrix, you will have more than enough material to write your discussion/conclusion during your regular writing sessions. The trick to keeping things manageable is to be judicious and *not make every possible connection,* only the most interesting and important ones. Here's a brief example of how your matrix will look:[1]

Table 10.1   Connecting My Findings to Other Findings

My Findings	Other Studies with Similar/ Convergent Findings	Other Studies with Different/ Divergent Findings	Connection . . .
Girls outperformed boys in the reading test	Jones, R. & Smith, E. S. (2010).	Jackson, R. B., Taylor, M. G., & Rubin, H. S. (2011). Mayner, J. T. & Post, I. E. (2011).	Jones & Smith obtained similar results, BUT measures were different. Jackson et al. and Mayner & Post found boys outperformed girls (the opposite of our finding), but they used the same measures we did.
No statistical differences between girls and boys in the math test for our sample		Jackson, R. B., Taylor, M. G., & Rubin, H. S. (2011).	No one found the same findings we did; Jackson et al. documented that boys outperformed girls. However, they had a much larger sample than our study did (could the significance be a function of sample size?).

EXERCISE 47—CONNECT THE DOTS: RELEVANT THEORY

TIME NEEDED: 10 minutes x session

MATERIALS NEEDED: Timer; visuals of your findings/results; the matrix you developed for Exercise 46

The discussion/conclusion section is *the* place in a manuscript where readers expect you to *interpret* your findings or results. Interpretation is not description: When you furnish the details and outcomes of a statistical test, you're describing what resulted from that test; when you list the themes you encountered in focus group interviews, you are describing what emerged from the data; when you tell the readers about the experimental group performing better than the control group, you're describing your experiment's outcomes. These are instances of *descriptive* writing, and they belong in the results/findings. In the final section in your report, however, you owe it to your reader to go one step beyond description and *interpret* your findings.

So what does it mean to *interpret* findings? If you consult a dictionary, you'll learn that the term *interpret* means "to give or provide the meaning of; explain; explicate; elucidate" (http://dictionary.reference.com/browse/interpret). And this is precisely what you must do with your findings: Tell the reader what they mean, explain why you may have obtained these (but not other) results, and clarify what these findings point to, what they *suggest*.

In this exercise, you will practice explaining *why* you obtained the results at hand. When attempting to explain *why* you got these results, you should make an effort to connect those thoughts clearly to the theory available in your field. The *why* question is theoretical—and the most important contribution your study can make is to the theoretical thinking in your field.[2] I won't have time to develop the topic here. For now, you'll have to trust me, as well as many other scholars who say contributions to theoretical thinking are invaluable.

This exercise, therefore, helps organize your thinking around the theoretical connections you may want to present to readers:

1. Set your timer for 10 minutes.

2. Using the matrix you developed for Exercise 46, add a column titled *theory* or *theoretical framework* and begin listing—for each salient finding you've chosen to discuss—which theoretical perspectives (or well-established theories) might help readers understand that particular finding. If your purpose

Table 10.2 Connecting My Findings to Theory

My Findings	Other Studies With Similar/ Convergent Findings	Other Studies with Different/Divergent Findings	Connection . . .	Theory	My Thoughts About Connection With Theory
Girls outperformed boys in the reading test	Jones, R. & Smith, E. S. (2010).	Jackson, R. B., Taylor, M. G., & Rubin, H. S. (2011). Mayner, J. T. & Post, I. E. (2011).	Jones & Smith obtained similar results, BUT measures were different. Jackson et al. and Mayner & Post found boys outperformed girls (the opposite of our finding), but they used the same measures we did.	Attention Deficit Theory	This theory discusses in detail how gender moderates reading ability.
No statistical differences between girls and boys in the math test for our sample		Jackson, R. B., Taylor, M. G., & Rubin, H. S. (2011).	No one found the same findings we did; Jackson et al. documented that boys outperformed girls. However, they had a much larger sample than our study did (could the significance be a function of sample size?).	Math Anxiety Theory	This theory proposes that test anxiety related to mathematics affects both genders equally.

was to test a certain hypothesis, list the theory from which the hypothesis was derived. In this new column, write the theory's name along with relevant sources/citations.

3. Now add one more column to the matrix to capture your thoughts about how the findings relate to that theory: how the results can be explained by that theory, or how they support or disprove it. Use a bulleted-list approach. Later, you will develop your bullet points within the text. Here's how the matrix will look at this point:

EXERCISE 48—GUIDE YOUR READER INTO THE FUTURE

TIME NEEDED: 10 minutes x session

MATERIALS NEEDED: Timer; visuals of your findings/results; the same matrix you developed for Exercises 46 and 47

Once I learned the importance of discussing my own findings, not veering off into tangents, and connecting those findings to other research or theory, I had little difficulty writing more in-depth discussions/conclusions. But they still lacked a crucial element. I rarely, if ever, answered the question most people ask after reading a study's report: *So what?* It wasn't until reviewers began calling my attention to this gap and colleagues started asking, *Now that we know this, what do we do with the information?* that I began to focus on the *implications* of my study, implications for current practice and future research.

Here's an example: Two colleagues and I studied health educators working in the United States (Chen, Kwok, & Goodson, 2008; the study was part of the first author's dissertation). We wanted to know how likely health educators were to adopt genomic competencies into health promotion research and practice. Genomic competencies comprise a set of skills and knowledge about public health genomics.[3] In our sample, we documented a rather low likelihood of adopting genomic competencies: Only 29.3% of participants in our study said they would probably adopt these skills and knowledge.

Well . . . so now we know. Health educators in the United States are not keen on engaging in public health genomics tasks in their practice. "Too bad," some would say, and "Who cares?" others might add. So, which is it? Is it too bad, or should we not even care? *So what?* Is there something we should do, something we should propose, something we should be concerned about?

In that study, a specific concern guided the inquiry—whether health educators in the United States knew about the developments in genetics knowledge and felt prepared to incorporate such knowledge into their practice. Because we had this specific concern, we *had to* address the implications of our findings, the *so what* of the results. As we learned in the study that three factors directly affected U.S. health educators' intentions to adopt genomic competencies, we made specific recommendations and highlighted precise implications related to these factors. Here's what we said:

The model [we tested] points to 3 important intrapersonal factors that directly affect intentions to adopt: awareness, attitudes, and self-efficacy.

Because these factors can be influenced through educational strategies, relevant training for health educators should gain priority among tactics to improve the public health workforce's capacity for public health genomics. Our study suggests, in particular, that attitude is the strongest predictor of likelihood: therefore, training focused on forming professional attitudes toward genomics should receive special attention. (Chen et al., 2008, p. 1655)

Addressing the *so what* question allows opportunities to call the field's attention to specific needs and to highlight areas of study needing more attention, requiring better quality research, or demanding closer scrutiny of measures, analyses, samples, or theory. In the example above, we made a specific appeal for practitioners to develop training emphasizing positive attitudes toward genomics.

This week's exercise, therefore, will help generate points for discussion regarding implications of your findings and recommendations for practitioners or researchers concerning your topic.

1. Set your timer for 10 minutes.

2. Examine the visuals depicting your findings, the thoughts you captured in your matrix, and what you've drafted so far for the discussion section.

3. Ask of your most salient findings: *So what?* What will people in the field be able to do with this information? Brainstorm your answers, using brief wording and short phrases.

4. If appropriate to your topic, divide your brainstorming list into three columns:

So What . . .	So What . . .	So What . . .
For Practice?	For Future Research?	For Theory?

5. Add these three columns to the matrix you've developed thus far, and spend 10 minutes each practice session this week brainstorming ideas to include in each of these columns.

6. Use your regular writing sessions to draft the discussion based on the points you raised in the matrix. You will find that the biggest challenge you now face is keeping the discussion section to a manageable size. If you had almost nothing to say in the discussion/conclusion before, now you'll likely have too much! Here's the matrix displaying the three new columns:

Table 10.3   Implications for Research, Theory, and Practice

My Findings	Other Studies With Similar/ Convergent Findings	Other Studies With Different/ Divergent Findings	Connection . . .	Theory	My Thoughts About Connection With Theory	So What . . . for Practice?	So What . . . for Future Research?	So What . . . for Theory?
Girls outperformed boys in the reading test	Jones, R. & Smith, E. S. (2010).	Jackson, R. B., Taylor, M. G., & Rubin, H. S. (2011). Mayner, J. T. & Post, I. E. (2011).	Jones & Smith obtained similar results, BUT measures were different. Jackson et al. and Mayner & Post found boys outperformed girls (the opposite of our finding), but they used the same measures we did.	Attention Deficit Theory	This theory discusses in detail how gender moderates reading ability.	Teachers need to be aware of gender differences when teaching this reading program.	Because fewer studies found similar results, more research should be done with samples similar to ours to confirm the validity of our findings.	Our findings lend support to the Attention Deficit Theory because gender did act as a moderator of reading ability in our sample.

EXERCISE 49—CONFESS LIMITATIONS

TIME NEEDED: 10 minutes x session

MATERIALS NEEDED: Timer; visuals of your findings/results; the draft of your paper so far

Most research reports include a brief paragraph or two discussing the limitations or problems that *may have affected the findings*. Notice, I wrote *brief* because readers are not interested in *all* the problems, setbacks, or frustrations you may have faced during your project. They are not the least bit interested in how long it took to get the study approved by the university's IRB (Institutional Review Board) or how long it took to get your measurements calibrated. I know . . . it's quite disappointing to realize no one really cares. But readers *are interested* in why you had planned to collect 560 usable surveys but received only 250. Because such a reduction in your sample size can seriously affect your findings (e.g., you may lose the ability to perform inferential statistical analyses) you should report this problem—and what you did to handle it—in a brief "limitations" segment.

No study is perfect, so there will always be something to say about the problems you faced and the solutions you developed. Nevertheless, many authors leave writing about the limitations for the very last minute and, due to time constraints, tend to rush through it—almost like a Catholic charging into a confession booth, blurting out, "Forgive me, father, for I have sinned," and leaving as quickly as possible. Not that the confessor needs to know the details of your sins, no. My point is that rushing through a description of your study's limitations doesn't allow you to reflect on them, on what you may have learned from them, on what you might do next time to prevent their reoccurrence. Many limitations sections in research manuscripts read like a quick, I-can't-wait-to-get-out-of-here confession, offered merely for convention.

This week, therefore, the exercise will help you spend time reflecting on your study's limitations by listing some of the problems you faced while conducting your study, along with the solutions you implemented. Readers who might want to replicate your study will benefit substantially from learning about the difficulties you faced and the solutions you implemented.

1. Set your timer for 10 minutes.

2. Referring to the drafts you've already generated describing your study, the findings, and the implications, list all the problems or difficulties that come to mind when thinking about the project. Don't worry about not recalling many of the problems: You'll remember the most important ones as you return to the list several times this week.

3. As you jot down your problems, assign a code to each one: Problems that may have influenced the outcome or the results get coded "Y" (for "Yes, they may have affected results"). The problems that would not have influenced the outcome get an "N" ("No, would not have affected results"). Once again, I recommend you use a table or matrix format for listing the problems. You will end up with a list looking somewhat like this:

Table 10.4   Study Limitations

Problems/ Limitations Faced	Affect Results?	Solutions Employed	Strengths
1. Problems hiring the research staff for the project. This led to a delay in starting.	N		
2. Problems defining the conceptual model—couldn't decide between two models.	Y		
3. Response rate from survey was low.	Y		
4. Didn't have time to pretest the survey questions.	Y		
5. Didn't have enough in the budget to print the report in color.	N		

4. Did you notice I have two more columns on the matrix? After you develop the list of limitations, coding them as Y or N, begin to list the solutions you employed to deal with the limitations.

5. In the last column, you should list the positive characteristics of your study that counterbalance the negative ones. As you develop your limitations list, it becomes really important to offset negatives with positives: Yes, your study is far from perfect and it had all these problems, *BUT* it makes all these contributions other studies don't make. Despite limitations, the contribution remains useful and solid. In your matrix, therefore, attempt to identify at least one positive characteristic of the study that compensates for each limitation listed.

Much like interpreting your findings, pointing out the positive contributions is something *YOU MUST DO FOR* your readers. Don't expect them on their own to view your study in the same positive light as you do, especially if you *end* your paper discussing its limitations: You should keep in mind that people remember best what they read last. Do you want readers to remember only your study's problems? Of course not! You want them to remember all the positive contributions your study makes! Therefore, be careful to balance presenting problems with presenting contributions. No, I'm not talking about merely describing the solutions to the problems you encountered. I'm talking about opening the readers' eyes and helping them see the big picture: what your study brings to the scientific dialogue about this topic *as a whole,* despite its problems. That's the function of the last column in my example matrix. So, when it's complete, your matrix will look something like this:

Table 10.5   Study Limitations and Strengths

Problems/ Limitations Faced	Affect Results?	Solutions Employed	Strengths
1. Problems hiring the research staff for the project. This led to a delay in starting.	N	—	—
2. Problems defining the conceptual model—couldn't decide between two models.	Y	We asked a panel of experts which model would be best.	This is the first study to use a theoretical model to study the topic.
3. Response rate from survey was low.	Y	But, typically, response rates are low for online surveys. We avoided generalizing from our sample.	Rates were low, but this is the first study of its kind, with this population.
4. Didn't have time to pretest the survey questions.	Y	We ran the data we collected through several tests of validity and reliability to check whether we collected the data we wanted to collect.	Even though we didn't pretest, the post-hoc statistical analyses revealed the data were valid and reliable (at above-average levels).
5. We didn't have enough in the budget to print the report in color.	N	—	—

Notice, I didn't bother writing a solution for the problems I will not report in the text (the ones tagged N in the matrix).

Paul J. Silvia (2007), in *How to Write a Lot,* presents a similar perspective about limitations. He cautions: "Don't merely raise your study's limitations—raise them and *then make a good case for why they aren't as grim as they look*" (p. 89; emphasis added).

By practicing this balancing act in your discussions, readers and reviewers will have the appropriate perspective and appreciation for your results and will value your study even more!

Notes

1. Please note that I've invented all the information—authors' names, findings, and theories—in this and the other tables in this chapter to function as simple examples.

2. If you want to learn more about why a contribution to theory is, arguably, the most important one a study can make, read *Theory in Health Promotion Research and Practice: Thinking Outside the Box* (Goodson, 2010).

3. Genomics refers to the complex system of interactions among individual genes and among the genes and their environment (Chen & Goodson, 2007).

References

Belcher, W. L. (2009). *Writing your journal article in 12 weeks: A guide to academic publishing success.* Thousand Oaks, CA: Sage.

Chen, L. S., & Goodson, P. (2007). Entering the public health genomics era: Why must health educators develop genomic competencies? *American Journal of Health Education, 38*(3), 157–165.

Chen, L. S., Kwok, O. M., & Goodson, P. (2008). U.S. health educators' likelihood of adopting genomic competencies into health promotion. *American Journal of Public Health, 98*(9), 1651–1657.

Goodson, P. (2010). *Theory in health promotion research and practice: Thinking outside the box.* Sudbury, MA: Jones & Bartlett.

Goodson, P., Buhi, E. R., & Dunsmore, S. C. (2006). Self-esteem and adolescent sexual behaviors, attitudes, and intentions: A systematic review. *Journal of Adolescent Health, 38*(3), 310–319.

Huff, A. S. (1999). *Writing for scholarly publication.* Thousand Oaks, CA: Sage.

Silvia, P. J. (2007). *How to write a lot: A practical guide to productive academic writing.* Washington, DC: American Psychological Association.

Teodorescu, D. (2000). Correlates of faculty publication productivity: A cross-national analysis. *Higher Education, 39,* 201–222.

Chapter Eleven

Exercise for Writing Abstracts

Summary

Think About It . . .

EXERCISE 50—Write an Abstract in 20 Minutes

A short saying often contains much wisdom.

Sophocles (497–406 B.C.)

Think About It . . .

You may never have stopped to reflect on the value of the abstract in a journal article or a research report, yet I'm *sure* you have read countless abstracts and relied on them to decide whether to continue reading a manuscript in its entirety. How important is an abstract, then? Paul J. Silvia's (2007) advice to writers summarizes it well: "Most readers who come across your article will see **only the title and abstract,** so make them good" (p. 81; emphasis added).

But what makes an abstract *good?* How do we write one?

Abstracts are wallet-size portraits of the big picture reported in your manuscript. I'm not sure wallet-size portraits exist any longer, but a few years ago, before digital cameras and smartphones, they were very popular. When families had their pictures taken, they usually received one large print to frame and several smaller photos that would fit in a wallet.

Abstracts function precisely as these wallet-size photos did: Whatever is portrayed in the big image of your manuscript appears in the smaller image, the abstract, proportionately shrunk in size. And because, in essence, the abstract is simply a miniature of the larger text, if you already have developed or drafted the main text, it's easy to generate its miniature.

Keep in mind, there are several types of abstracts (varying in length as well as style), because abstracts serve slightly different purposes in different documents. The specific aims section in a grant proposal functions, at times, as an abstract of the entire document. Longer in length than journal article abstracts, specific aims sections are commonly restricted to one single-spaced page containing all important highlights of your proposed plan: a brief background, purpose, rationale, specific goals/objectives, procedures, and expected outcomes. Some reviewers assigned to read your proposal may have the opportunity to read only that summary page, nothing else. For this reason, some scholars view the specific aims section as functioning more like an abstract than an introduction.

A different type of abstract is the executive summary found in the technical reports written for funding agencies. These are longer (sometimes a couple of pages), but their purpose is to condense the information in a lengthy report to a bulleted list of its main points (especially the findings). Again, it is not uncommon for funding agencies to circulate only the report's executive summary among interested parties.

In some areas of study, abstracts submitted for conference presentations are published in a professional group's flagship journal (in addition to appearing in the conference's program booklet). These abstracts—limited to 250 words, on average—must stand alone in representing your manuscript because they may be all of your study that most researchers ever read (and sometimes cite).

Regardless of which type of abstract you are writing, it is important to bear in mind that the abstract also serves to convince the intended audience of the manuscript's *value*. Kendall Powell (2010), for instance, wrote in an article for *Nature:* "Some editors suggest that 'winning over' a skeptical editor, reader or reviewer should be the ultimate goal of any paper's abstract" (p. 874).

And how do we effectively win over our readers or reviewers? Powell (2010) provides an interesting tip:

> Leslie Sage, an astronomy editor at *Nature,* says authors should avoid an abstract structure that says: we did X, which told us Y, and has implications for Z. Instead, he says, start with why a reader should care about learning more about Z and then explain how this work furthers that goal. (p. 874)

Abstracts focusing less on description and more on argument (or on answering, *why should the reader care?*) are more difficult to write, but with practice and observation you can learn to grab your reader/reviewer with your abstract. It's best to begin by writing descriptive abstracts; once you master writing this type of abstract, move on to writing the more argumentative ones.

Even though abstracts may serve slightly different functions and have different formats, the underlying purpose is always the same: to provide a brief, summarized account of your report—what you found and what it means. Therefore, a good abstract has two main characteristics: (1) It is formatted appropriately for its purpose and intended audience, and (2) it contains the main elements from the bigger picture of your study, your report. I state the obvious, therefore, when I claim abstracts are very important and you should pay close attention to these characteristics as you write them.

Regardless of which type you choose (descriptive or argumentative), you should always try to write your abstract *last.* When you write it after completing the draft of your entire manuscript, you can write it quickly. It is much harder to write an abstract before your report is drafted (and some scholars would say doing so is ethically questionable). Another reason for writing the abstract last is you can devote time exclusively to polishing the abstract, without worrying about the rest of the paper or report. Silvia is correct: More often than we care to admit, the abstract will be the only portion of your work read by most readers. You should, no doubt, spend extra time and effort to make your abstract shine!

In this section, I offer an exercise with two faces: one for authors whose manuscripts have already been drafted and one for authors who have not yet completed their draft but must write an abstract for an upcoming conference presentation, for instance. In the first part of the exercise, you can truly pull an abstract together in about 20 minutes. The second part, too, can be done quickly if you know what you're going to say, but it will take a bit longer than 20 minutes.

Research Shows . . .

Grzybowski and his colleagues (2003) reported on the successful implementation of a writing group, developed specifically to support physicians' writing for publication, in the Department of Family Practice at the University of British Columbia.

The writing group met in the evenings, at participants' homes, over a period of 36 months (23 meetings total). Between 3 and 10 faculty attended each of the meetings. Over the course of the meetings, 50 writing projects were reviewed, 12 of which were published in indexed journals (p. 195).

According to the authors of the study: "The seven most frequent attendees increased their publications as first author from one publication over the 3 years prior to the writing group to 10 publications over the first 3 years of the writing group" (p. 195).

The authors also explain how writing groups offer a valuable, nonthreatening environment and provide feedback as well as social support for writers. Their review of the extant literature also highlights the benefits of participating in writing groups to improve teaching as well as publication productivity.

EXERCISE 50—WRITE AN ABSTRACT IN 20 MINUTES

TIME NEEDED: Two 10-minute sessions

MATERIALS NEEDED: Timer; the file containing the draft of your complete manuscript

If you have drafted most of your manuscript, complete these steps:

1. Set your timer for 10 minutes.

2. Go through your entire manuscript and highlight each paragraph's key sentence with a bright color.

3. Format your abstract to reflect the exact same structure as your manuscript. Most commonly, you would write the abstract with the following sections: introduction, purpose, methods, results/findings, and discussion/conclusion. If you're not following this structure, select the first-level headings from your manuscript and use *those* as headings for your abstract.

4. You may have time for only items #2 and #3, above, in your first practice session. If so, use the 10 minutes in your next sessions to do the remainder of the exercise.

5. Choose several key sentences you highlighted in color. Copy and paste them into the appropriate sections in your abstract.

6. Once you have several original key sentences in the introduction section, for instance, come back and clean that text: Keep only the most important statements, edit for flow and connection, remove unnecessary ideas, and always remember the word count or other restrictions placed on the abstract (space is always limited!).

The main point is to not have to rewrite anything for the abstract except, perhaps, to add a few connections and transitions as needed. Most of the text is ready. Also note, repeating yourself here is not a problem. You may use the same words as in your text to write the abstract: This is not self-plagiarism; it's a faithful miniature snapshot of your study. The closer the two align in their wording, the better.

Caution! Do not place any figures, tables, or citations in the abstract. The abstract must stand alone. It cannot refer to anything outside itself. (The exceptions to this rule are the specific aims page in grant proposals and, at times, reports' executive summaries, but use of visuals or citations must be limited, even in these types of abstracts.)

If you have not yet drafted your manuscript, complete these steps:

1. Set your timer for 5 minutes.

2. Choose a structure for your abstract (introduction/purpose, methods, results, and discussion usually works well). Think of each section as a drawer in a filing cabinet.

3. Begin brainstorming a bulleted list of key ideas you want to have in the abstract (for now, don't worry about what goes where). Write them as brief statements, short sentences. Spend about 5 minutes doing this (setting up the structure and generating your key ideas).

4. Set your timer for another 5 minutes.

5. For the next 5 minutes, begin placing the ideas you generated into their appropriate drawers. Spend this time organizing what you have and noting what you omitted.

6. During the next practice sessions this week, spend time editing or organizing your drawers and generating the items you still need to fill them. Pay attention to the word limit. If you find you have too much text, use the suggestions for cutting down text I offered in Chapter 6, Exercise 26.

By week's end, you should have a clean, edited abstract. It will have taken longer than 20 minutes because you had no text to draw from, yet it shouldn't take you more than a couple of hours total—distributed across several days.

Example

Below, I provide two examples of abstracts published in professional journal articles. The first one is descriptive; the second is argument based. Both can be labeled good abstracts.

Descriptive Abstract

Objectives. We examined US health educators' likelihood of adopting genomic competencies—specific skills and knowledge in public health genomics—into health promotion and the factors influencing such likelihood.

Methods. We developed and tested a model to assess likelihood to adopt genomic competencies. Data from 1,607 health educators nationwide were collected through a Web-based survey. The model was tested through structural equation modeling.

Results. Although participants in our study were not very likely to adopt genomic competencies into their practice, the data supported the proposed model. Awareness, attitudes, and self-efficacy significantly affected health educators' likelihood to incorporate genomic competencies. The model explained 60.3% of the variance in likelihood to incorporate genomic competencies. Participants' perceived compatibility between public health genomics and their professional and personal roles, their perceptions of genomics as complex, and the communication channels used to learn about public health genomics significantly related to genomic knowledge and attitudes.

Conclusions. Because US health educators in our sample do not appear ready for their professional role in genomics, future research and public health workforce training are needed. (Chen, Kwok, & Goodson, 2008, p. 1651)

Argument-Based Abstract

The development of advanced writing skills has been neglected in schools of the United States, with even some college graduates lacking the level of ability required in the workplace. . . . The core problem, we argue, is an insufficient degree of appropriate task practice distributed throughout the secondary and higher education curriculum. We draw on the power law of skill acquisition, the role of deliberate practice in expert performance, and the uniquely intensive demands that advanced written composition place on working memory to make this case. A major impediment to assigning enough writing tasks is the time and effort involved in grading papers to provide feedback. We close by considering possible solutions to the grading problem. (Kellogg & Whiteford, 2009, p. 250)

References

Chen, L. S., Kwok, O. M., & Goodson, P. (2008). U.S. health educators' likelihood of adopting genomic competencies into health promotion. *American Journal of Public Health, 98*(9), 1651–1657.

Grzybowski, S. C. W., Bates, J., Calam, B., Alred, J., Martin, R. E., Andrew, R., et al. (2003). A physician peer support writing group. *Faculty Development, 35*(3), 195–201.

Kellogg, R. T., & Whiteford, A. P. (2009). Training advanced writing skills: The case for deliberate practice. *Educational Psychologist, 44*(4), 250–266.

Powell, K. (2010). Publish like a pro: Prolific authors and journal editors share how to get manuscripts noticed, approved and put in print. *Nature, 467*(14), 873–875.

Silvia, P. J. (2007). *How to write a lot: A practical guide to productive academic writing.* Washington, DC: American Psychological Association.

Afterword

I wish thee as much pleasure in the reading as I had in the writing.

Francis Quarles (1592–1644)

I wish I could end this book the way Paul J. Silvia (2007) ended *How to Write a Lot:*

> This book is over; thanks for reading it. I enjoyed writing this book, but it's time for me to write something else, and it's time for you to write something, too. (p. 132)

Yes, although it is time for *me* to write something else, I'm sure *you* have already written quite a bit as you practiced the exercises in this book. Congratulations! You persevered, remained patient, and practiced, practiced, practiced. You are well along the path to stress-free academic productivity, and because of your dedication to your writing, I can't end this book in quite the same way as Silvia ended his.

Instead, I want to offer a few parting words, a last bit of encouragement, one final dose of support to help you sustain the momentum you established. I offer these words as a wish list of hopes I will always harbor for your writing career.

So, for you, my reader . . .

- My first wish is that this book has inspired you to master your academic writing. I wish you many days in which you feel completely in control of the writing process, in which the ghost of writing anxiety that haunted you in the past has been defeated and your writing is free from stress and anxiety.
- I hope you have begun to apply the principles in the POWER model, to practice all the exercises and tips, and to adapt these principles and practices to your own preferences. That's the beauty of POWER, after all: ideals and

foundations that render it a flexible model, allowing you to take control of your writing in ways that are meaningful to *you*.

- I hope that through careful and habitual practice, writing is becoming such an integral part of your daily routine, you rarely, if ever, ask, "When will I ever get any writing done?"
- I hope you are writing significantly more than you were before you practiced with this book and that you have written thousands of words *TO THROW AWAY!!!*
- I wish you many years of paced, powerful, and productive writing, finishing projects *ahead of your deadlines,* realizing you *can tackle that monstrous writing project* for which someone volunteered you, and knowing you can *keep publishing at a steady pace.*

Above all, my deepest desire is that you never forget Peter Elbow's (1998) gentle reminder, with which he ended *Writing With Power:*

> The precondition for writing well is being able to write badly and to write when you are not in the mood. (p. 373)

Because writing badly is *necessary,* according to Elbow, I also must wish you lots of bad writing and many days when, despite your desire to be at the beach, you sit down and write one or two sentences, somehow. As you tackle those days of poor writing and foul moods that certainly will come, count on me to be thinking of you, your struggles and successes. I will be cheering for you as you move ahead, and in so doing, I will be reminded that although the task is difficult, the persistence pays off for everyone. I will certainly be experiencing my own share of days full of bad writing and lack of motivation; so remember me once in a while, too! If along the journey you wish to share your successes, need encouragement, or require help, please contact me by e-mail at goodsonworkbook@gmail.com. It would be an honor to meet you, hear your writing story, and perhaps learn that my wishes for you have indeed come true!

Now . . . this is, *really,* I promise . . . THE END.

Well . . . maybe not, perhaps merely . . .

THE BEGINNING?

References

Elbow, P. (1998). *Writing with power: Techniques for mastering the writing process* (2nd ed.). New York: Oxford University Press.

Silvia, P. J. (2007). *How to write a lot: A practical guide to productive academic writing.* Washington, DC: American Psychological Association.

Appendix

Additional Resources

S ome of these resources I already cited in the book, but many of them you will not find in the text. This is, by no means, a comprehensive list, merely a guide to the many tools available to help you write more, write better, and sustain your productivity. Enjoy!

To Feed Your Writing Soul

Babic, G. V. (2008). *Words to inspire writers*. Australia: F. C. Sach.

Cameron, J. (1997). *The vein of gold: A journey to your creative heart*. London: Pan Books.

Conner, J. (2008). *Writing down your soul: How to activate and listen to the extraordinary voice within*. San Francisco: Conari Press.

Dillard, A. (1989). *The writing life*. New York: HarperPerennial.

Fadiman, A. (1998). *Ex libris: Confessions of a common reader*. New York: Farrar, Straus, & Giroux.

Goldberg, N. (2005). *Writing down the bones: Freeing the writer within* (2nd ed.). Boston: Shambhala.

Lamott, A. (1994). *Bird by bird: Some instructions on writing and life*. New York: Anchor Books.

Rosenblatt, R. (2011). *Unless it moves the human heart: The craft and art of writing*. New York: HarperCollins.

Weinstein, L. A. (2008). *Grammar for the soul: Using language for personal change*. Wheaton, IL: Quest Books.

Zinsser, W. (2009). *Writing places: The life journey of a writer and teacher*. New York: Harper.

To Maintain Motivation

The Academic Ladder: http://www.academicladder.com
Author Aid: www.authoraid.info
Cohen, S. (2010). *The productive writer: Tips & tools to help you write more, stress less & create success.* Cincinnati, OH: Writer's Digest Books.
Emphasis on Excellence: www.meggin.com
Get a Life, PhD: http://getalifephd.blogspot.com
Gray, T. (2005). *Publish & flourish.* Springfield, IL: Teaching Academy, New Mexico State University.
Gray-Grant, D. (2008). *8 1/2 steps to writing faster, better.* Vancouver, BC: Highbury Street Books.
King, S. (2000). *On writing: A memoir of the craft.* New York: Pocket Books.
McCloskey, D. N. (2000). *Economical writing* (2nd ed.). Prospect Heights, IL: Waveland Press.
Publication Coach: www.publicationcoach.com
Rankin, E. (2001). *The work of writing: Insights and strategies for academics and professionals.* San Francisco: Jossey-Bass.
Saltzman, J. (1993). *If you can talk, you can write: A proven program to get you writing & keep you writing.* New York: Warner Books.
Silvia, P. J. (2007). *How to write a lot: A practical guide to productive academic writing.* Washington, DC: American Psychological Association.
Steel, P. (2011). *The procrastination equation: How to stop putting things off and start getting stuff done.* New York: Harper.
Text and Academic Authors Association: http://www.taaonline.net

To Learn More

Belcher, W. L. (2009). *Writing your journal article in 12 weeks: A guide to academic publishing success.* Thousand Oaks, CA: Sage.
Clark, R. P. (2006). *Writing tools: 50 essential strategies for every writer.* New York: Little, Brown.
Day, R. A., & Gastel, B. (2006). *How to write & publish a scientific paper* (6th ed.). Westport, CT: Greenwood Press.
Elbow, P. (2012). *Vernacular eloquence: What speech can bring to writing.* Chicago: Oxford University Press.
Elbow, P., & Belanoff, P. (1999). *A community of writers: A workshop course in writing* (3rd ed.). New York: McGraw-Hill.
Germano, W. (2008). *Getting it published: A guide for scholars and anyone else serious about serious books* (2nd ed.). Chicago: University of Chicago Press.
Hartley, J. (2008). *Academic writing and publishing: A practical handbook.* New York: Routledge.
Huff, A. S. (1999). *Writing for scholarly publication.* Thousand Oaks, CA: Sage.

Johnson, W. B., & Mullen, C. A. (2007). *Write to the top! How to become a prolific academic.* New York: Palgrave McMillan.

Nash, R. J. (2004). *Liberating scholarly writing: The power of personal narrative.* New York: Teachers College Press.

The Purdue Online Writing Lab (OWL): http://owl.english.purdue.edu/

Sabin, W. A. (2010). *The Gregg reference manual* (11th ed.). New York: Career Education.

Wolcott, H. F. (2009). *Writing up qualitative research* (3rd ed.). Thousand Oaks, CA: Sage.

To Handle Specific Issues/Tasks

Bruce, S., & Rafoth, B. (Eds.). (2009). *ESL writers: A guide for writing center tutors* (2nd ed.). Portsmouth, NH: Boynton/Cook.

Casagrande, J. (2010). *It was the best of sentences, it was the worst of sentences.* New York: Ten Speed Press.

Cook, C. K. (1985). *Line by line: How to edit your own writing.* Boston: Houghton Mifflin.

EndNote (reference/citation manager): http://www.endnote.com/

Graff, G., & Birkenstein, C. (2006). *They say; I say: The moves that matter in academic writing.* New York: W. W. Norton.

Grammarly (grammar checker): http://www.grammarly.com

Lanham, R. A. (1999). *Revising business prose* (4th ed.). New York: Longman.

Lucid Chart (free mind-mapping software): www.lucidchart.com

O'Conner, P. T. (2009). *Woe is I: The grammarphobe's guide to better English in plain English* (3rd ed.). New York: Riverhead Books.

OneLook Reverse Dictionary: http://www.onelook.com/reverse-dictionary.shtml

Rafoth, B. (2005). *A tutor's guide: Helping writers one on one* (2nd ed.). Portsmouth, NH: Boynton/Cook.

Readability Calculator: http://www.online-utility.org/english/readability_test_and_improve.jsp

RefWorks (reference/citation manager): http://www.refworks.com

Roget's Thesaurus of English Words and Phrases: http://poets.notredame.ac.jp/Roget/

Sharp, C. (2000). *A writer's workbook: Daily exercises for the writing life.* New York: St. Martin's Griffin.

Sullivan, K. D., & Eggleston, M. (2006). *The McGraw-Hill desk reference for editors, writers, and proofreaders.* New York: McGraw-Hill.

Truss, L. (2003). *Eats, shoots & leaves: The zero tolerance approach to punctuation.* New York: Gotham Books.

Visual Thesaurus: www.visualthesaurus.com

Weston, A. (2009). *A rulebook for arguments* (4th ed.). Indianapolis, IN: Hackett.

Williams, J. M. (2010). *Style: Ten lessons in clarity and grace* (8th ed.). New York: Pearson/Longman.

To Display Data in Graphs, Figures, and Tables

Gapminder: http://www.gapminder.org

Miles, M. B., & Huberman, A. M. (1994). *Qualitative data analysis: An expanded sourcebook* (2nd ed.). Thousand Oaks, CA: Sage.

Nicol, A. A., & Pexman, P. M. (2010). *Displaying your findings: A practical guide for creating figures, posters, and presentations.* Washington, DC: American Psychological Association.

Nicol, A. A., & Pexman, P. M. (2010). *Presenting your findings: A practical guide for creating tables* (6th ed.). Washington, DC: American Psychological Association.

Tufte, E. R. (2001). *The visual display of quantitative information.* Cheshire, CT: Graphics Press.

To Have Some Fun

Conrad, B., & Schulz, M. (Eds.). (2002). *Snoopy's guide to the writing life.* Cincinnati, OH: Writer's Digest Books.

Dr. Wicked: http://www.drwicked.com

Nichols, S. E. (2009). *I judge you when you use poor grammar: A collection of egregious errors, disconcerting bloopers, and other linguistic slip-ups.* New York: St. Martin's Griffin.

Author Index

Subject Index